The Trawler

2022

The Poems in *The Trawler 2022* were selected from poems posted on the Gloucestershire Poetry Society (GPS) group Facebook pages, from June 2021 to May 2022, by the following.

Carol Sheppard
Jason Conway
Josephine Lay
Karlostheunhappy
Peter Lay
Tish Camp
Trevor Valentine

Throughout this anthology you will find a number of Haiku/Senryu etc., in response to haiku challenges set by Karlostheunhappy.

The Trawler

2022

Gloucestershire Poetry Society
Anthology of Selected Poems

Black Eyes Publishing UK

The Trawler 2022
Gloucestershire Poetry Society Anthology of Selected Poems
© Peter Lay 2022

Published 2022
Black Eyes Publishing UK
34 Stocken Close
Hucclecote
Gloucester GL3 3UL(UK)

www.blackeyespublishinguk.co.uk

ISBN: 978-1-913195-23-6

Editor: Josephine Lay
www.thegloucestershirepoetrysociety.com

Cover design: Jason Conway, The Daydream Academy.
www.thedaydreamacademy.com

Introduction

It gives me great pleasure to introduce this anthology of poems trawled from the Gloucestershire Poetry Society (GPS) group Facebook pages.

The Trawler 2022 is the third and final edition in the trawler series, there was always only going to be three. In 2023, the GPS annual anthology will take a different form, details of which will be announced in due course.

Here are a further one hundred and eleven poems (posted between June 2021 and May 2022) by fifty different poets. Some of these poems may be rough first drafts, still in need of polishing (we have only lightly edited) but never the less they are of sufficient value to be included within these pages. Some are by published poets, and some by people who have just begun writing, being published for the first time, but each poem has an element: a style, voice or passion that called to us as we read it.

We hope you'll enjoy these poems penned and posted with enthusiasm for the written word. These poets come from all parts of Britain and Ireland, from France, Germany and the Netherlands, and some from as far away as the United States, Australia, India, Togo and the Caribbean.

The GPS is once again thrilled to work in conjunction with Peter Lay of Black Eyes Publishing UK, and with Jason Conway of The Day Dream Academy on this *The Trawler 2022.* All profits go towards the funding of the Gloucestershire Poetry Society.

Josephine Lay   October 2022

Contents

13   **Anthology** – Josephine Lay

15   **A billion** – Matty Blades
16   **A Celtic Dream** – Jason Conway   *(#haikuchallenge)*
17   **A circle of bone** – Drea MacMillan   *(#haikuchallenge)*
18   **A cold, pale azure** – Vicky Hampton   *(#haikuchallenge)*
19   **A graceful ballet:** – Saly Aspden   *(#haikuchallenge)*
20   **another moon haiku** – Ivor Daniel   *(#haikuchallenge)*
21   **A Passing Storm** – Ann D Stevenson
22   **A single last star** – Josephine Lay   *(#haikuchallenge)*
23   **AT THE AIRPORT** – Chloë Jacquet
24   **Avebury: The Outer Circle** – Drea MacMillan
25   **A Wolf in Poet's Clothing** – Louise Longson
26   **A Year Like This** – Tish Ince Poet
28   **Basho and Buddha** – Karlostheunhappy   *(#haikuchallenge)*
29   **Behind The North Wind** – Charlie Markwick
30   **bitter over brewed tea** – Scott Cowley
31   **Bonfire '21** – Ivor Daniel   *(#haikuchallenge)*
32   **Bracing** – Z. D. Dicks
33   **Bring Me a Ladder** – Sue Finch
34   **CAFFEINE RUSH** – Marilyn Timms
36   **Cerberus Smited** – Jason Conway   *(#haikuchallenge)*
37   **Christmas** – Sue Hubbard
39   **CLOAK THE DAY IN DUSK** – Henry Farrrell
40   **Cloudless sky, smoothed blue** – Sue Finch   *(#haikuchallenge)*
41   **Collected walnuts** – Adele Ogiér Jones   *(#haikuchallenge)*
42   **Covid – Day 8** – Peter Lay
43   **Crown** – Nupur Chakrabarty   *(#haikuchallenge)*
44   **Cueva de las Manos, Argentina** – Vicky Hampton
45   **Diana and Dai** – Derek Dohren
47   **DISCO DOGS** – Devlin Wilson
48   **DON'T BREAK DOWN** – Ann-Marie Kurylak
49   **Electrical Wire** – Darcey Royce

50   **Evening** – Carol Sheppard   (*#haikuchallenge*)
51   **evening** – Amy Bingham   (*#haikuchallenge*)
52   **First Day Back** - Lou Hotchkiss-Knives
53   **Foraging last days** - Adele Ogiér Jones   (*#haikuchallenge*)
54   **Forever Marvellous** – Nick Lovell
55   **Forevermore** – Matty Blades
57   **forgotten and forgettable** – Scott Cowley
58   **Ghosts** – Simon Townsend
60   **GHOSTS OF THE DANUBE** – M. Palowski Moore
61   **Half the sky** – Kuma San
62   **Heaviness** – Akondo Nouhr-Dine
63   **"Hello"** – Matty Blades
64   **Here is what I have so far!** – Nick Lovell
66   **Homeless** – Kelly Owen
68   **Hunt** – Nick Lovell
69   **HUNTING** – Doreen Baidoo
70   **I fall weightlessly** – Jason Conway   (*#haikuchallenge*)
71   **Ignorance Abyss** – Kezzabelle Ambler
74   **Imagination: Text** – Dane Ince
77   **I'm grateful, but there are still the lost** – Matty Blades
78   **In case of emergency** – Carol Sheppard
79   **Inhale** – Jason Conway   (*#haikuchallenge*)
80   **Insomnia** – Elvis Gregory-Sayce
82   **I polish shoes** – Tish Ince Poet
83   **{ It's All About You }** – Elvis Gregory-Sayce   (*#haikuchallenge*)
84   **It's a work in fucking progress!** – Scott Cowley
87   **Ittai** – Kuma San
88   **I Was A Teen** – Rebecca Mo
89   **Let the past dissolve** – Sally Aspden   (*#haikuchallenge*)
90   **Metafalls** – Matty Blades
91   **Moon** – Karlostheunhappy   (*#haikuchallenge*)
92   **My Mate Steve** – Derek Dohren
94   **No body's home** – Kelly Owen
96   **On Commitment** – Drea MacMillan   (*#haikuchallenge*)

97   **Perhaps, he thought** – Jon Collins   *(#haikuchallenge)*

98   **Playing** – Katherine Grace Hyslop

99   **Postcard** – Carol Sheppard

100   **PRAYER OF THE ZODIAC NIGHT 15TH APRIL 2022**
                    – Karlostheunhappy

102   **Rampage** – Nupur Chakrabarty

103   **Real Bed** – Tish Ince Poet

105   **Refugee** – Kuma San

106   **Rule of Three** – Morgan Rye

108   **SAINT SARAH THE PATRON SAINT
OF THE ROMANI PEOPLE** – Raine Geoghegan
- Her Names are Many
- Shrine at Saint Marie de la Mer
- Lucky 'eather
- The One
- Know My True Face

111   **S.A.D: Seasonal affective disorder** – Jason N. Smith

112   **Sewn on the bias** – Tish Ince Poet

114   **Shroud** – Louise Longson

115   **Silk** – Jason Conway   *(#haikuchallenge)*

116   **Silver Service** – Sue Hubbard

117   **Skye** – Derek Dohren

118   **snowdrop drink the sun** – Karlostheunhappy   *(#haikuchallenge)*

119   **Snowdrops at imbolc** – Adele Ogiér Jones   *(#haikuchallenge)*

120   **Sorceress** – Darcy Royce

121   **SPIRIT DANCERS** – M. Palowski Moore

122   **STANDING OVATION FOR THE WOMAN**
                    – Agu Chinedu Ejorh

123   **star burst haiku** – Matty Blades   *(#haikuchallenge)*

124   **STARS KEEP VIGIL** - Karlostheunhappy

125   **Swinging** – Sue Finch

126   **The Coin** – Sue Finch

127   **the day ahead of me** – Ivor Daniel

128   **The doorway in my mind is a metaphor** – Jon Collins

129   **The jasmine flowers** – Louise Longson   *(#haikuchallenge)*

130   **The Mellowing** – Darcy Royce

131   **The Olive Tree** – Charlie Markwick

132   **There are no more tears** – Jason Conway

133   **THE REAL THING** – Clive Oseman

135   **There's something to be said** – Jon Collins

136   **The traveler** – Louise Diamant

137   **The vlogger, the baker, the mortgage maker** – Morgan Rye

138   **Timber Cries** – Trevor Valentine

139   **To Cheer Up Digger Down** – Julian Roger Horsfield

142   **Vomit** - Scott Cowley

143   **WAITING** - M. Palowski Moore

144   **waiting waiting waiting** - Scott Cowley

146   **Walking Meditation** – Sally Aspden

147   **Weals** – Charlie Markwick

148   **woken from the dead** – Carol Sheppard   *(#haikuchallenge)*

149   **Words that cannot be** – Marilyn Timms   *(#haikuchallenge)*

150   **woven to match snow** – Adele Ogiér Jones

151   **The Poets**

The Trawler 2022 is an Anthology.
The word Anthology came from the Greek -
Anthos meaning flower or blossom
Legein meaning to gather or collect.

Josephine Lay

Anthology

All this year we trod the paths of words
scrolled the posts of poems
collected voices, ideas, passions
that shone out of our screens.

We heard your voices,
fragile and delicate, fresh as early cherry,
were attracted to your ideas
as butterflies to buddleia

We followed the scent of passion
rose and jasmine,
though pricked by thorn or tangled by stem
we were happy to be caught.

Wild poems flowered
like thistle and buttercup
as prickly and as obstinate
yet we dug them up.

We twisted all blooms into this garland
and now, at the close of the year
we shine a bright torch on those
we are about to hear.

Matty blades

A billion
stars in a single drop,
an ocean full of worlds
web weaved across galaxies vast,
linking together the universe

B¿@d€ 18.8..2021

Jason Conway

A Celtic Dream

Cerridwen shapeshifts
Her matriarchal wisdom
Lessons in moonlight

Taliesin floats
Leather-wrapped grain sent to sea
Whispers over sand

Nine moons spurn legend
Great poetry for valleys
Echoes through the vale

The silver crone hangs
Watches over fertile ground
We stargaze spellbound

(#haikuchallenge)

Drea MacMillan

A circle of bone
Pitted centre, smooth edges
gnawed by the night's teeth

(#haikuchallenge)

Vicky Hampton

A cold, pale azure,
birds beneath its low-slung sun.
Winter's dressed to kill.

(#haikuchallenge)

Sally Aspden

I'm having a go at this month's haiku challenge. Here's one of my favourite moments watching Gloucester's seagulls (I have a strange fondness for the seagulls):

A graceful ballet:
gulls gleam white against black sky
circling slowly.

(#haikuchallenge)

Ivor Daniel

another moon haiku

pearlescent fruit gum
overhead you glow   the last
one in the packet

(#haikuchallenge)

Ann D Stevenson

A Passing Storm

Erasure poem from text in 'The House by the Marsh' by William Blyghton.
With kind permission of William and his publisher, Panacea Books.

The storm gone,
stillness settled,
the damp air quiet.

On the beach
bric-a-brac
tossed onto shingle.

A freshness
in the air,
the sea at ease.

Her moods
mattered not,
all seemed intact.

Small branches, broken,
lay upon the ground,
that was all.

Josephine Lay

A single last star
there, on the edge of darkness
like a hope fading.

(#haikuchallenge)

Chloë Jacquet

AT THE AIRPORT

Tangerine women shiver
in outfits fit only for their destination.
The bar is a thundercloud
of stags and hens all outdoing
each other's drinking and singing.
Groups of lads regretting
their previous night's decisions
bend their bodies in an attempt
to lie across jutting armrests.
Football shirts and wide-brimmed hats
wander in packs drinks in hand.
Suits seek sockets for laptops.
Parents appease child-gods with offerings.
An unintelligible announcement
booms from the ceiling.
A swarm of people rises
like flies to head to a gate.
A new swarm comes in
and settles in their place.

@ChloeJPoetry

Drea MacMillan

Avebury: The Outer Circle

An enamelled, nicotine stained sky hangs above huge sacred teeth.
Emerging from gums of green grass,
rooted deep in their chalky jaw,
thirty resolute boulders bite into the scenery,
baring themselves in an open mouthed grin.

Warm rain licks the rocks with it's gentle tongue.
Wet sheep wander between the toothy gaps,
fluffy, resembling chunks of saliva coated, masticated, bread.
Spinachy lichen clings, like fragments of trapped food,
to the monolith's long eroded ridges and troughs.

At the gumline toothpick-sized tourists pilfer plaquey pebbles
from the Pagan consecrated earth which now recedes,
exposing buried sarsen rock and dirt the colour of aged spit.
Decayed and pitted, bleached by once worshiped divine light,
chipped and tarnished these prehistoric towering stones still stand

The wind breathes through this monumental mouth
humming ancient songs that whistle through cavities and cracks.
Picked at for centuries, drilled and chiselled with crude tools
Mutilated in the name of cleanliness and purity.
These crooked canines and mystical molars smile on.
.

Louise Longson

I've been on a really excellent poetry course today (run by Wendy Pratt). I discovered how hard I find it to be original in writing about walking in the woods in winter. This is what came out...

A Wolf in Poet's Clothing

I am being watched in the woods; stalked
by the ghost of Robert Frost.

He is dogging my footsteps
like a hungry wolf and preying

on my mind. His graceful winter similes
echo in mine, I have no other reason

or rhyme. His poem has locked me in
its jaws and will not let me go.

I can only follow this well-travelled road
through an avalanche of metaphors of snow

to where the fairy-lights of dewdrops hang on
sugar-dredged pines and all my words hibernate

in a mental thicket, lovely, dark and deep,
lying dormant until the end of time.

Tish Ince Poet

A Year Like This

I am a return, echo call
to broken familial hearts
kept away
stay away
breathe

I am all in my being
with or without
like sunshine pleats and rays
or the grey, thunderous pour
of 'unfair' cry
in calamitous rain

I am the struggle, the ache
the grief, laden in layers
of ham sandwich trays
carried to empty front rooms
of baking kitchens
the muffin mix
spooned by a child
like thick drops of love
sticky-stuck-lick
(sweet taste)

I am paint on canvas
colour, brushed through
yellows, the blue-purple hues
wet finger prints
hands joined in pink

I am doorstep waves
a quivering lip
watching this curl, in his

the toddler, the slip, trip-grip
the fingers prised loose
like koala bear cling
finding dummies and crisps
hearing tyres, the gravel,
and goodbyes' sting

I am this year recalled
this year - these tears
I am this.

Karlostheunhappy

Basho and Buddha
talk of the cherry blossom
without moving lips

(#haikuchallenge)

Charlie Markwick.

Behind The North Wind

Barbara was showing me work she had contributed to an exhibition "Behind The North Wind": https://www.shetlandarts.org/our-work/exhibitions/behind-the-north-wind. In her uniquely laconic way she said. "You should write a poem!"

The black and inky sky
punched through by star and broken moon,
I hear a howl and cry.
She launches South the slicing wind
and I prepare to die.
Scalpel cold will flay my flesh.
Will the salty heat of my
spilt blood satisfy her bloody lust?
I strive with mind and eye
to see behind the North Wind's spite.

There with leaping heart I spy
the white hot threads, the ropes of hope
that merge to help and fortify
the people in those Northern lands.
The energy they claim, does that deny
us the stuff of life? This can't be so.
Their skill is just to multiply
the good in all and give to each of us a share.
So all they do is amplify
the treasure found in most of us.

So when I hear the howl I'll try
not ask, what drives the cold North Wind
as now I know the reason why.
She flees the warmth and good in Northern lands.
She fears the way that they defy
her will, her rush to bleed them dry.

Lerwick 15/06/18

Scott Cowley *(aka Rusty Goàt the Poet)*

bitter over brewed tea

monday morning, coffee shop sitting
a mug of wonky-white
(americano without milk)
stirred left with a spoon

coffee shop, thinking
it's unsweetened
so does it really need stirring?

I'm wondering...
did I get out of the darkside
of the bed this morning?

sitting, still anticlockwise stirring
contemplating whilst inward breathing
stirring, slowly exhaling, still sitting

the inhaling feels grey and cloying
exhaling has the taste of bitter
over brewed tea, unsweetened
(i'm no heathen)

contemplating
over thinking

i'm wondering...
did I get out of the darkside
of the bed this morning?

Ivor Daniel

Bonfire '21

Firework images,
nose of gunpowder, damp leaves,
ripe Westminster sleaze.

A Guy in my Dad's
old suit frowns sadly - neither
suffered fools gladly.

(#haikuchallenge)

Z. D. Dicks

Bracing

The horizon was a faded dappled peak
where light brimmed up a blossom
of dewey leaves turned static crunch
that plunged to ash under hoof crush

A brisk wind rose to a bucolic height
folded as flour into bleached blue
it cried unbound for snow in ether
wound down sunshine into a glutter

Ice and water clattered in hues
like a maelstrom of colour held in air
that drifted pulses without labour

Where bombs, in the distance, dropped
scattered bundles of metallic perfume
away, thundered a taste of summer.

Sue Finch.

Bring Me a Ladder

Send me a kite, I called to the wind
I want to watch that ribboned tail unfurl.

Bring me a ladder, I said to the sea,
because I once painted a sky exactly like this

and there are angels up there.

Call the flying fish to rainbow my ascent.
Let each salted rung hold for just one step.

Marilyn Timms

CAFFEINE RUSH

We bumped into each other
outside Costa.
I apologized for my clumsiness
took her inside for an impromptu cappuccino.
Milk froth, white as sea spray, beaded her upper lip.
I'm a mermaid, she said, and I believed her.

Why not?

Waist-length hair moving with an inner life
like a sea-grass forest.
Eyes, luminous as the moon's trail
across an ocean.
Her voice, sibilant as tides at midnight.
A soft, fishy, iridescence to her skin.

I was totally, painfully in love.

The mermaid left as suddenly as she had appeared.
I watched the sway of her hips as she moved lithely
between tables, thought of a retreating tide
oozing around rocky outcrops on a beach I knew.
Sea-blue, shot-silk skirt clung possessively
to taut, muscular thighs, halted above shapely calves

that led my eye down to

slender ankles
and ....
long narrow feet!
A siren shriek from the coffee machine
introduced me to reality.
What mermaid has legs?

Where was her tail?

The fumes of first love dissipated as rapidly the steam
that writhed around the barista and his infernal machine.
I felt confused, humiliated, grief stricken, cheated.
My adored one was a liar.
No mermaid she –

it was patently obvious
that she was a Selkie.

Jason Conway

Cerberus Smited

Cubs howl shell shocked
Their masters worship sky fire
Ares smites Cerberus

Ritual sermon
Zeus' bolts synthesised joyously
War dogs terrorised

Blind obedience
By guarded growling gentry
Punished for pleasure

All hail the fifth
November brings night chaos
It's not in our nature

Children gaze starstruck
Tradition a forced religion
As the wild cowers

(#haikuchallenge)

Sue Hubbard.
From my second collection, Ghost Station (Salt)

Christmas

I try to imagine
If he came back,
pressing his pale, half-forgotten

face against the cold pane,
looking in through shadows
of lamplight and rain

at the smeared glasses, the empty
bottles of wine and fallen needles
of Christmas pine.

The deserted street silent
In December dark, the curtains
at each window drawn tight

to stop the bleeding out of private light
and he watching, as we recycle pain,
wondering why, again and again,

we don't learn love's declensions.
Yet if he stayed a moment longer
he might find, among the smell

of discarded orange rind,
the odour of unmade beds
and drying sheets, of coal dust

and yellow chrysanthemums
wilting in a jar, a shifting sense
of what has changed –

dilute as a homeopath's dose
invisible in the pale liquid's glass –
into a glimmer of something

precious: like a lost ring,
a pebble, a rusty key,
a question mark of fallen hair.

Henry Farrell

CLOAK THE DAY IN DUSK

The night---
Of days, it ever shall:
And I sing with the kiss of the twilight-
'though its verse purports not to show the moonlight

As springs from the clouds in lay!
Their infant dew;
The light fleet of little tears
Dictating chillingly, bereft cares:

Alas! as the fall besmears the nights glory,
Unanticipatedly dictates to me! joyful slumber---
As strives there! a continent in keep
Of pregnant cells, lending their excess...
of burdensome weep

Sue Finch

Cloudless sky, smoothed blue
holds a printed moon.

(#haikuchallenge)

Adele Ogiér Jones

Collected walnuts
this day early autumn week
sun's gold promises.

(#haikuchallenge)

Peter Lay

Covid - Day 8

Josephine and I finally caught Covid in April 2022.

Coughing is very draining
especially late in the evening
like yesterday
Just when you thought
it was over
you are doubled over
sucking in air
to throw it out
cough, cough, cough.

Nupur Chakrabarty

Crown

This Haiku tells how the soaring desires of a person invites gloom and murk.

A crown on his head
scintillating dream towers
unfolding darkness.

(#haikuchallenge)

Vicky Hampton

Cueva de las Manos, Argentina

Cueva de las Manos in Argentina is named for the hand paintings stencilled in collages on the rock walls between 7,300 BC to 700 AD. Scholars believe the stencils were made predominantly by women.

Through time we came here,
on good days and bad, together,
chatter-full with stories. And alone,
at the menses, when the blood's
current was as the hunted bison.

Through time we came here,
laid our left hands one upon another,
stitched our mark to the rock.
We took the caves contours
softened hardness with woman's design.

Through time we came here,
puffing a pollens' millennia from reed
and mouth, the trees' hard coats chewed
to paste – the good earth's colours
patterning stone and bluff.

Through time we came here,
blowing blacks and reds down the length
of our smiles, ochre through gossip,
our hands turning white stone
to the outline of nations.

Derek Dohren.

Diana and Dai

work in progress this one, though it may have disappeared up itself...

I was chatting in the pub
Diana and Dai were Christians.
They'd been dead
as a dodo
before they were born,
had then died
to be born again
so that when they died again
they would be saved from death
by a man who had died
long before Diana and Dai
were born,
had died,
been born again
and would die again.

Diana and Dai had been dying
to get to Heaven
in each of their lives.
Dai told me that one day
after he had died again
(after having been born,
died, and born again),
he believed he would be
born again again.

Dai hoped to be able
to share dialogue
with the dead again
and born again again Diana
and tell their four
dead again grandparents
in Heaven,

now born again again,
(after having been
as dead as dodos,
born,
died,
born again
and died again),
all about it.

I asked Diana what she thought.
She said, "call me Di,
everyone else does."
I said doesn't that get confusing.
And if looks could kill ...
I offered to buy another round
but Dai declined.
"It's dead in here", he said
I said, "Hang on, let me get a pen
and write this down.
There's a killer poem in this."
etc etc etc

Devlin Wilson

DISCO DOGS

Crazy glue calico mainbrace
That's how I choose to train my whippet
Black crepe covers the skylight
Disconnects me from lupine recovery service
Last four incidents of cat malpractice
Ferried funicular to front door
Sub post mistress ages less fast post mortem
Streaming frankincense sub sound cloud
Murder in the garment district
Cut to bruised indigo skies
Hunched detective threads clues on tip off
From jockstrapped giant par excellence
Unleash the whippets now cry havoc
Disco dogs amidst marsupial din
Ensures ensuing wombat harvest…enough

Ann-Marie Kurylak

DON'T BREAK DOWN

I soldier on, marching on
Carry on cos that's what's done!
Yes I'm tired, yes I'm worn
World weary and teary
But I can't stop.
I'm told I can cry, but don't break down
You've gotta go on
You can't just stop
That's not how it's done, not now
Not ever, gotta be superman, or woman, or both
Be brave, take it head on
You're strong!
Oh god please stop!
Yes I know, I'm supposed to take it all in stride
Cry in the shower or behind closed doors
Then wipe away the tears, oh no, nothing's wrong
I'm fine, I'll say, I'm getting on
While each worry and fear gnaws like a rat on my tired old bones.
Maybe I'm too young to be this tired
Should have been born in the dark ages, I'd have already expired
Maybe I'm not fighting for my life, not like it was then
But I've been fighting for his, and our life together
The sweat on my brow and the ache in my back
Is nothing to stop for, not if we want our life back on track.
So I'll just lie down for a minute, maybe turn off the light but
I can't close my eyes, I can't give in to rest
This is a challenge I have to best, so they tell me.
But I can't stop and stay here
I have to get back to the fight
Just give me one moment....please....and shut off the light

Darcey Royce

Poets get inspiration from the smallest of gestures, from the least notable words, from people who most of the time don't even know they touched my heart in ways for a new poem's birthing, materialized on paper, feelings I recognize and put in rhythm and rhyme...

Electrical Wire

He could not make sense of it,
at all, why,
when before,
that well known itch, the hunger,
easily satiable thirst - sooner or later, would rose from his core to take
over all the senses and hers,
for a brief moment - he never needed more than that - satisfy the
profane, the animalistic in him, and tame the same beast in her,
turned into an empty throbbing, aching wire,
etched to their skin,
conductor of a certain kind of electricity - hers,
coiled like a snake around his chest,
a slippery slope of first times,
this one's different,
this one's strong,
and clever... thoughts hammering, cascading down his waking hours
all consumed energy,
cold and hot sweat rolling down his icy temples - hot lava flow,
this woman knows when to squeeze,
when to release,
hold him in, put him out to chill,
drive his breathing fast, or slow..
halt his breathing altogether,
for a brief moment or eternity,
until he'd explode..
in anticipation..
how!? when, why...
he could not make sense of it,
at all.

Carol Sheppard
Here is my attempt at Karlostheunhappy haiku challenge

Evening

Log fire sparks scarlet
Curtains open, moon dazzles
Hot star-gazing pie

(#haikuchallenge)

Amy Bingham

evening

Time travel at night
Bright stars and dreams will guide you
Light from years gone by.

(#haikuchallenge)

Lou Hotchkiss-Knives

First Day back

Eight a.m., the light floods in
The long corridors stretch empty
A ghost ship mourning your absence
a door slams, somewhere
Echoes in the distance

Crossing the yard and noticing
Your classroom plunged in the dark
I remember the days
I used to day-dream
Watching the nesting birds

On Wheatridge Lane
sparrows and swifts
once sat chirping on power lines
Long gone
Last week I turned fourty

What happens now
on September evenings ?
Google searches void
A Ronoake of a man
inexplicably gone

There are other Heavens, I know
There will be other smiles
Are you even alive ?
And could I take another blow ?
The night never winks nor replies.

Adele Ogiér Jones

Foraging last days
came upon elderberries
rosehips forest gems.

(#haikuchallenge)

Nick Lovell

Forever Marvellous

The theatre lies deserted,
The audiences long gone,
Yet in that deep dark silence,
Forgotten voices echo on.
The passion and the laughter
Their eloquence and grace.
Beside the soul of every person
That ever visited this place.

The boxes stare down sightlessly
At the darkened stage so bare
But even in abandonment
Words whisper though the air.
Ghosts of past performances,
Soft, haunted overtures
As actors from a thousand plays
Bow to memories of applause.

Matty Blades

Forevermore

Another gig tonight comes a voice from the corner, a man sat in a top hat with a leather strap, gold teeth shining in the light

Curse of the vampires he said under his breath, then laughed so hard he nearly choked before retiring into the dark

I had an omen this morning of a blood red moon, crows feasting on rotten corpses, bats eyes a'flame with ancient darkness, and the eerie sound of the howling of the wolves

I looked to see where the man had gone, then on the table I see his card, 46 Blade Crescent, then poof! It just burst into flames

This played on my mind as I left the bar I heard shuffling down the street, screeches from something unholy seemed to be stalking me, a chill rushes up from my feet

As I walked a little further, the man in the hat was dancing in the street, singing, come dance till you're drained, dance forevermore for the God's of rock "n" roll, I was intrigued to listen to something new In the distant sky a shadow loomed large, wings the span of the moon, curse of the vampire was hanging low saying we're open from midnight to noon

What band could play for 12 hours straight? Super human maybe? This I'll have to see, then as the door drew ever nearer, I walked through and got my stamp

The room was dark, red lighting adorned the walls, behind the band were flames and as the music pumped right through me, a rush I could not contain

The singer bit the head off of a bat, then it turned into a headless man, I freaked and tried run, but far too late, the bands games have just begun

The beautiful singer turned pure white, leaped and held me down stripping off my clothes, biting and teasing, drinking and sinking, I didn't know if I was coming or going but it sure felt good on the bone

My mind went blank dreaming a dream about a cave, there was an inscription written in fiery script, I touched the wall it opened up, my eyes began to glow

When I awoke the band were in full swing, blood dripping from the ceiling, but I, still alive, felt like I was dying

I could see their veins throbbing begging to be sucked dry, I felt a hunger like nothing I ever felt before, my throat tightened my mouth was dry as hell

I tried to lunge and take a feed, but chained to my new master, she drew her sword and teazed her blade across my neck, oh for a moment to be set free

Looking to my master with wanton eyes, her teeth still dripping with blood from her previous prize, the body lay lifeless beneath her feet, I pang for just a taste

My teeth like sheers, claws like knives ready to slice flesh and drain them dry, my first I slashed across the face, the band went wild the sound of death

Sucking it dry I had my fill, then wings like blades cut through my skin, transforming me from mere man to a god, I was coming into my own

I joined the pack that day for sure, a nomads life 5000 years, I see empires rise and empires fall, but never had a thirst like man for war I'll probably be here till the end of time, dissolve with the earth when the sun goes boom, so think of me as you swig a bear, stalking somewhere forevermore.

M.Blades
Copyright 21.4.22 ©
W{}rd$ fr{}m B¿@de-z ©

Scott Cowley *(aka Rusty Goàt the Poet)*
What would you like for breakfast?
Words… my simple reply.

forgotten and forgettable

the people you remember
are they remembering you too?
a trace indelible?
memories clawing, scratching, screaming
regrettable, forgotten and forgettable?

names, some of which i've lost.
events, which have run through my fingers,
the sands of time.
delirium, disjointed, gutter slime.

as you left that place, unknown.
each carefully placed step,
a hobnail boot on broken glass.

the pages you ripped out,
chapters, paragraphs, sentences erased.

life; delible

Simon Townsend

Ghosts

Ghosts of faces
Mostly unseen
People in the places they'd
once been
The old man walking to pick up his
papers
Little kids out on mischievous
capers
The young woman riding a bike along her
usual route
The business man looking sharp in a
pinstripe suit
The chap who's daily exercise involved a
bacon roll
At the end of each and every
daily stroll
People there at first glance then gone
are you seeing them through happenstance
Snapshots
Images that once
vivid
Like a Polaroid picture
Soon Fade with
time
But memories
persist
The kind couple in the corner shop that sold you
penny chews
An old friend not gone long but still here
for you
The couple hand in hand immaculately
turned out

The old boy on the corner who used to
holler and shout
How can these images exist then go in the
blink of an eye
Like replays of footage from the
minds eye
Ghosts of faces
Mostly unseen
People in places they'd
once been

M. Palowski Moore (Silver Lion Poet)

GHOSTS OF THE DANUBE

In less than two months, approximately 20,000 Jews were massacred, murdered on the banks of the Danube River. More than three thousand Hungarian and Jewish citizens lost their lives on the Danube Bank during the Arrow Cross Terror. Before the executions they were ordered to remove their shoes.

I came
To the murky waters
To feel
The wanton waves
Of the River Danube
To experience
To understand
The legacy
Of the souls
Who left
Their shoes on the Bank.
The wind carried voices
Pleading, screaming, agony
Gunshots, silence
Spirits falling, floating
Away from
The phantom stage.
I cried standing there
The river swelled
The dark water
Came to my feet.

Kuma San

Half the sky
For International Women's Day

Women hold up half the sky ♡
though this has been hotly denied,
through the years and eons of time,
it is women who birth all blood lines.

So beware these sacred keepers of life,
the ones who keep to paths of less strife,
the ones who know and whisper to trees,
they hold and believe the dreams we all need.

The birthers, the mother's, the carers of others, the listeners, the
bleeders, the life-giving feeders...without them your life would be
nought but a hole in the ground and a free-floating thought.

Kuma x

Akondo Nouhr-Dine

Heaviness

On the throne
of needs
Beyond and bellow
all heeds
Within the claws and canine
A tender lamb
Vied and leaked by U-rope felines
Chews the cud and cramps
The fleshy and blood flushed thigh
Cramps the sub-soil
To feed a people rough
With car-house-money broil

Africa, the freaky angel
Among canine sits in prey
In wait of all freaks and marvels,
They say.
The plumb-winged angel
Chews the cud of the past
A fertile past,that rings the bell
For a hungry future, in fast
Expectations to be fed
But bled in lethargy,
By an incest with a global world.

Matty Blades

"Hello"

no voice returns
but a stare of indifference,
mine indignance, one of dispair, somewhere
yet nowhere, who would but care?

The streets they held no hope for me,
but pain it thrived inside,
insomniac, or just too cold to sleep in the
black, hiding out in the park at night

Nick Lovel

Here is what I have so far!
Not sure it's finished yet... Not sure it's fit for purpose even...

We study the arts, the sciences, humanities.
Teach manners, elocution and other inanities
Learn how to drive, how to ride, how to draw,
Practice at medicine, dentistry, law
But for all the things taught, all the lessons gone by
Never once do we consider the correct way to die.

See, it's the one thing that's certain, no way to avoid,
That day we take our last step into the void,
When we cash in our chips to buy one final round
When life's last illusions finally come crashing down
Should I be stoic and silent or wail, weep and cry?
How on earth can I find out the right way to die?

Will there be tubes, anaesthesia, syringes and nurses,
Or cold hard wet tarmac, with traffic and curses?
(Just spare me the poets with their bloody verses)
Will I be sane or will I be raving?
Will my heart be stout or will I be craven?
Will I be gross and bloated? Will I be fit and spry?
When I discover the secret of just how to die?

How quick will it be? Will I struggle and linger
Until all movement is gone, aside from one finger?
Should I be fully conscious or simply sedated?
Will it be all of a sudden or anticipated?
Could I summon a Priest, Imam or Rabbi
Would they help me discover the best way to die?

The thought just won't go from the back of my head,
After all, what's the point, I will still be just as dead,
And the way that I pass will hardly sum up my life,
Nor be the way I am remembered by my children and wife

Still I continue my quest, from this search I won't shy
Until I find out the correct way to die!

Last words are important, for posterity's sake
So, "oh fuck" or "Bollocks" are probably a mistake,
Should I prepare a speech, a phrase or word,
But if no-one's around it will just go unheard?
It's become an obsession, there is no way that I
Can give up until I find the right way to die.

It's always unspoken, so coated in mystery,
Yet everyone's done it throughout human history
Though nothing is known, There's one thing that's certain
The performance is over, it's the final curtain
So perhaps take that last bow, to the audiences' cries
And maybe, that might be the best way to die!

Kelly Owen

Homeless

I'm crying
Shocked at the kindness
Beautiful on the inside
As rough exteriors causing blindness

A little mindfulness
For the hero's who go unspoken
Sleeping in doorways
Because their worlds became broken

Don't ask me to do this as spoken
I'm slightly broken as well
These people still smile
While living your worst fear
Your hell

All these beautiful people
With journeys to tell
But you're all thought of as they pray
You walk past a man in a sleeping bag
With a doorway to stay

They're not in the way
They're not causing you harm
They put up with coldness
They don't raise alarm

They remain calm
As they just fight through each day
Praying for the next hot meal
Or wondering if they'll be kicked
From that doorway

Today I cry
For beautiful inside
Rough on the out
Who still hold their smiles
While living in doubt

They know what life is about
Every smile they take in
Showing kindness to others
To them feels like a win

So just begin
To open your eyes
Real people with real problems
As they silence their cries

The sleeping bag
The hunger
The love
This bares no lies

Nick Lovell

Hunt

I once slew a metaphore
I tracked it long, two days or more,
Over mountain, river, moor
Until in rich and leafy glade
It confronted me with mighty roar,
It leapt, attacked,
claws ripped, teeth snapped
Knocked me flat upon my back
Its weight a thousand of tons of coal
Its pelt black as a devil's soul
Its mouth a scarlet pit of hell
Its breath a most disgusting smell.
It reared to strike again and I
Drew my knife and with a cry
Of fear thrust forth my trusty blade
Prayed that it was strongly made
That it wasn't poorly aimed
I didn't want the creature maimed.
My strike was true, the metaphore
Collapsed onto the fern strewn floor
It fixed me with its emerald eye,
Then in its high pitched voice asked "Why?"
It gave a sigh then asked again
Its voice now weaker, full of pain
I assumed the question was not rhetorical
"Your death, dear Sir, was purely allegorical"

Doreen Baidoo

I'm going to try again.
I woke up a month ago and wrote a poem.
Then I got up, made a pot of coffee and sat down with my laptop and eventually found
GPS. This shows how powerful and magic-full a poem can be. I almost renamed it The
spell. Well here it is with it's original title

HUNTING

I need to find my tribe
That tribe of poets
Or writers, willing to share
Willing to bare their souls
In a well-held space
To put it out there
Inside soft padded walls

A place to scream your pain
Gently
And have it land
On embracing ears
And encouraging eyes

I know you are out there
So.........
I'm going to
Gather up my courage
And go a-hunting

Jason Conway

I fall weightlessly
An old leaf desiccated
Ground hungers my fall

(#haikuchallenge)

Kezzabelle Ambler
I collaborated with Benji Dotan-Creative to make this film for an international art exhibition 2020 Vision: Living Rooms & Loo Rolls Online

Ignorance Abyss

I took daily risks on earth's behalf as I awoke,
stretched and laughed, consuming from the moment I rose.
Yawn, pee, fart, wiped my arse with wet wipes,
peachy clean but not green.
Air freshener sprayed to mask,
blue chemicals swirled down the loo,
when fresh lavender, lemons or vinegar would do.
subconsciously I was saying,
'I don't give a shit about the planet.'

Tore off more perforated tissue
the world's sliding issues begin.
Ran the tap, pumped the manufactured soap onto my skin;
the plastic dispenser read
'Sea Breeze – anti bacterium'
Sleepily standing at the sink
I think in my hazy delirium
'don't we need some bacteria?
they're our natural fighters'.

Squeezed the man-made tube of minty paste
- more unsmiling waste,
my convenience at the earth's inconvenience,
I'm in a rush, 'must invest in a bamboo toothbrush'.
I sink into my chair, a cool drink from the Frigidaire
poured from the coated cardboard container with the
carefully designed non-drip synthetic spout that makes no mess.
Not impressed by that irony
watching, the juicer sits idly.

Parents join the mile-high club
of toppling piles of disposable nappies

that sit in landfills for generations
before they even start to break down.
We're the clowns building a foundation of crappy plastic,
not fantastic or so easily disposed of.
Let's break this strangling chain
and rein in our expendable choices
for our children's children who are voiceless.

Watching on we couldn't feel finer in our prettily designed
packaged products collecting life's flow from our vaginas.
Tampons, tubes and padding regularly bought
and discreetly disposed of but to where?
Let's face facts they're so heavily taxed they'll keep quiet
about the cheaper greener alternative out there.
Save money and our earth by purchasing a mooncup once
then we'll leap into sports fads smiling like all the ads
say we do, at 'that time of month'!

Maybe tomorrow I'll sort out the glaring changes needed
around me but less tomorrows for the creatures of the sea
with no voice or choice in the matter
in the clatter of human fools.
We rule from a school of thought that ignores mountains
of minuscule plastic droplets that bejewel and fuel our lives.
Never satiated by the rainbow of mass produced forms
we've 'cleverly' created, invented for our short-term fix
and delight or just to 'save time'.

Life's magpie shinier things climb, glossing over
and distracting us, sweeping challenging
world problems under the carpet or into the sea.
Cesspools of waste slowly seeping, creeping into our
beautiful waters drowning in our throw away lifestyles.
Even the food we eat is being affected,
tainted by our expulsions, daily chemicals,
sprays and gasses as the masses turn a blind eye,
relaxing in the green room of life.

Animals try desperately to search for ground
to forage and survive in our tarmacked,
slabbed and civilised infrastructure.
Our 'green and acquiescent land'
rains smog polluted tears upon us,
we're slowly but surely wrecking and wreaking
havoc on our world
Ssshhh - enough earth stuff - mums the word,
more mantras of not knowing but we know.

We console ourselves that at least we recycle in this
daily cycle but we know deep down we can do more,
just a decision away, second by second, day by day,
no matter what our mates say;
we can amend life-long habits,
learnt behaviours passed down,
refraining from this daily drain –
the earth's running on empty
and yes, I know I drove here today.

I'm not perfect in any way, it's a challenge, life's balance.
But I'm learning and discovering
natural recipes and remedies for cleaning me from within,
my home, environment, my skin.
A daily warrior not worrier of shared tomorrows
on borrowed time, as precarious, precious
and delicate as that is.
We often fear change in our chosen unaware
let's start to care again in our bumpy love affair with life.

Kezzabelle Amber© 15.9.2018

Dane Ince

Imagination: Text

I am down a rabbit hole
Most definitely I am
I want that PINK cowboy suit
Them duds like fine to me
Look
I thought about this one word
On what was a blank page
Screen
Wall
 scream
Am I this
All of this
All of this one word
Silence
The cursor blinking
To show me where I am lost next
Here
Here
Here
Carved beach sand
BURR ON ETCHED METAL PLATE
I hold a salty branch
Watching what happens next
SWIM IN AN ACID BATH
I REMEMBER CASPER
PRINTING lithographs of brick walls
I am out of time now
I am not your mistress
Roses for a head pigeons on my stocking arms
I imagine a pipe
You see the pipe when I say I imagine a pipe
I imagine a tobacco pipe
You see a pipe

I imagine a pipe for smoking tobacco
I imagine
I burn my fingers lighting the pipe
Do you imagine my brief pain?
See the blank page
See the one word on the page
Both are in my imagination
Like the robot who stole your job
Fucking ATM
I knew one day
We would buy a device that does not move
But we still move
We watch what moves
See the movement on the device
The world fits into your pocket
The device moves with us
Everything is moving
Glendale, California
A corporation made a word
For what people will do
Anyway
Illustrators
Engineers
Architects
Lighting designers
Writers
Painters
Graphic designers
They work officially for an umbrella company
Imagination is work
designing
 building everything
 theme parks
 resorts
 attractions
 cruise ships
An and
of oars

Wide range of salaries
Potential for ideas
This is not a poem
It is words in random order
Radon gas cancer

Matty Blades

I'm grateful, but there are still the lost

As I stand looking out my door,
old and new memories flood my thoughts
The ghost's of many cold winter's past,
have come to rest easy this day at last

Outside it's grey and misty vision,
inside it's warm the smell of cooking
I still remember the struggle deep, all
those years feeding out the skips

Yes at times I do feel lost, when I look back at all that come to pass
I remember so much the sleepless nights, the tossing and turning a
demons fight

Walking for miles and miles I'd roam,
looking for drugs to numb the pain
I'd score the shit fix it in my vein,
frying what little brain cells I had left

But the change that now I've come to see,
is so much more than I'd ever believe
I'm free at last from that tormented past,
but so many still are paying the cost

Carol Sheppard

In case of emergency:

Don't call me.
I'm not free.
Call someone else instead.
I'm no good at spontaneity,
Surprises fill me with dread.
Switch off my phone, bolt the door,
I don't live here anymore.

Jason Conway

Inhale
Hold
Release

(#haikuchallenge)

Elvis Gregory-Sayce

Insomnia

I'm Awake

R U
On Social Media

My Mind
Bends N Weaves
Open All Night

Shackled By
Mind Of Will
Well Not Sleeping
No Sleep 2night

Up Watchin' Facebook Posts
In Commin' Tweets
Tick Tok Videos
Every 1's A Celebrate T
These Dayz

Green Tea Might Get
Me Off 2 Noddy Land
Used 2 When I Was
A Young Lad About 2
Tucked Up In Bed
With Big Ears

Can't Say That
Big Ears Now DayZ
It's All Gone Pete Tong
That's Rhyming Slang
4 A Bit Wrong

Wrong I Can't Sleep
2night It's Now
3am An Owl Hootz
That's Strange

Am I Hallucinating
Must Have Been
Those Mushrooms

I Picked In The Forest
Earlier 2day I'm Late 4 Work

I Must Have Fell A Sleep

Tish Ince Poet

I polish shoes

I took his shoes to polish, quickly
every step he takes in them
imagined as someone else's last
on TV, I reach for pixels of compassion
in the world, an apron and black wax

in a country, bombed
where shoes lay about
telling their blood tales
amongst bricks and glass
from feet that cannot be washed in oils
crucifying our histories
Jesus, barefoot walks amongst the debris

their sandaled feet are cut
brave, treading what might be
roads to refuge, trauma trains
chug full of their killing dreams
reaching boarders in their nightmare blasts
living thoughts of futures
hopes and grief

this war is, this week, wailing walls
long will this last, I polish
use all my energy
for these are shoes upon shoes
I want to clean.

Elvis Gregory-Sayce

{ It's All About U }

Countries In Pandemic
Countries On Fire
Countries @ War

Yet U Want A Holiday
2 Fly Away From Your Stress
How Ironic

(#haikuchallenge)

Scott Cowley *(aka Rusty Goàt the Poet)*

It's a work in fucking progress!

pull up a chair
sit a little closer
I have some words that you may want to hear...
it's not an insistence
just a humble open invitation

where should I start, what could I say?
i mean, oh my fucking days...
it's about time that the poetry paid!
(in reality, it never will)
the miles traveled
the bullshit endured, on that, I could say more...
the odd time that I've sworn, that this is the last one
the gig right here and now, is my swan song

sit a little closer
pull up a chair
don't be feared
it's just me, my borderline personality disorder
and my imaginary dog, called Geoff
that being said, the borderline
I've often questioned

forgive me a moment
i may have digressed
now, where was I going with this
ah yes, please sit and listen
if you wish...

with a deep chested breath
with hand up on left side of chest
trying to stay focused
tea, strong

toast, hot buttered
and a request that the language
doesn't come from the gutter...
but the poetry will always remain
the same acerbic, direct, brutally honest craft
"not under my breath" didn't signal that it was all over
that book, metaphorically speaking
is available with a alternative front cover

dust off the mic
hold the front page
sweep the stage
take the curtains back to the wings
it's not over until
until the fat lad sings

hand up on left side of chest
with a deep chested breath
pain that goes into arm and neck
complex cardiovascular, heart failure
with a pinch of unstable angina
the price I'm paying for questionable lifestyle choices?
or just a whole load of bad luck?
In all honesty it's more the likely the former

tea, strong
toast, hot buttered
dust of the mic
curtains back to the wings
acerbic, direct, brutally honest craft
"not under my breath"
didn't signal it was all over

forgive me
i have digressed

pull up a chair
sit a little closer

it turns out
that the reality is
this plot has a twist
which is still
a work in progress

Kuma San

I recently finished painting some glass panels for a dear friend. The process was totally new to me and the project has taken a few months to complete.
I have learnt a lot and enjoyed the focussed slowness of painting in this way.
I didn't realise until I'd finished how immersed I was in it all.
This poem is about that bit after I finished...it was a little weird. The feeling of slight dislocation is only just starting to fade.

Ittai

For Diana Tobin

It's quiet, I can hear myself breathe,
tired muscles smoulder, I slouch
on the floor, arms on knees,
eyes unfocused, vacant.

The silence is a relief, my head,
momentarily void of dialogue,
pounds with the pulse of blood,
this is an end, a completion,

The last leg of a long trek in to
the unknown, my cartography
of an unexplored land is over,
the painting is finished.

As I cleaned the last brush,
something big left the room,
a sense of loss dances with
relief in this void place.

Its the quiet after a party,
just you, the dark, memories
and the mess.

Kuma x

Rebecca Mo

I Was A Teen

I hold a fondness for these streets
Friendships formed, friendships ended
First kisses
Drags on shared cigarettes
Mum's left a pizza again
Tesco and back again
Sugar and schnapps
Shots of Archers, the sweetness hiding the taste of alcohol
Miles walked
Canal
Boys. And girls.
Fuzzy duck
Does he fuck?
Think of Maggie!
Swings we sat on, then we stood on
Queens and Kings of the playground
Fire, fire!
Secrets of school spill out of our mouths
Bats and carp
Christmas lights for charity money
Christmas carols for pocket money

Sally Aspden

Let the past dissolve.
Let go of future, and self.
See blossom glowing.

(#haikuchallenge)

Matty Blades

Metafalls

See cascading metafalls cause a tsunami of emotional release
Freedom is born within every word, only thing I found to bring me
peace

Hard pressed the scars left on pulp for the ages a timeless page
Remembering all those traumatic stages, face it and make a change

When the noose tightens at times I'm unable to find the words
Blinding visions plagues the mind, right then it feels like a curse

Invading every moment like a play list of my favourite songs
Watch me hit it on quick fire poems never finished micro filed

My mind thinks in rhythm and rhyme, rest relaxation and moan
Skipping words across the page, a blessing when you live alone

M.Blades
Copyright 9.5.22 ©
W{}rd$ fr{}m B¿@de-z ©

Karlostheunhappy

Moon

summer moon rises
not full, pale white, cut, unwhole
but still moon rises

(#haikuchallenge)

Derek Dohren

My Mate Steve

My mate Steve's got street smarts
he ain't no kind of a fool.
He doesn't care about what you read in books
nor that stuff you learn in school.
Sure, though he says he's been there on his holidays
it's true he can't spell Chihuahua
but that's not the kind of brain Steve's got.
I'm talking a different sort of mental power.

Some mates of my mate Steve
think the Earth is flat
and to hide it the world's governments have done a deal.
Though my mate Steve isn't having any of that
he'll tell you straight up, wrestling's real!

My mate Steve's got his wits about him
he ain't no kind of a fool.
He doesn't care about what you read in books
nor that stuff that makes you cool.
Sure, though he says he's saving for his pension
he spends his money on fags and booze
but that's just the kind of brain Steve's got.
He's walking a different mile in his shoes.

Some mates of mates of my mate Steve
think the moon landings were all faked.
They love all that 'Kubrik directed the films' intrigue.
Though my mate Steve thinks this is kind of half-baked
he'll tell you straight up, Spurs'll win the league!

My mate Steve's not some crazy buffoon
no kind of a fool is he.
He doesn't care about what the wise men say
nor the lessons of history.

Look, Steve's got his foibles and his quirks, I admit.
Sometimes I look at him
and he's as incomprehensible to me
as a steam engine enthusiast
or one of those people
who collects royal family memoribilia.
Don't get me wrong,
we all have our idiosyncrasies don't we.
Mine are particularly weird.
I like taking perfectly serviceable poems,
opening them up,
and shoving in verses
that have nothing to do
with anything that's gone before,
but I digress.

Some mates of mates of my mate Steve's mates
think the CIA are pulling all the strings
and the Illuminati is controlled by reptilians.
Though my mate Steve doesn't believe such things
he'll tell you straight, he's gonna win lotto millions!

Kelly Owen

No body's home.

Knock knock
Is anyone home
No answer today
Even though the lights are on
Where's the emotions now gone
Leave me alone

Now I'm an emotionless shell
No longer crying
This evening a complete mess
Feelings now dying
One fucked up state
Without even trying

Just everything now stripped away
One empty shell
Even the employment didn't stay
Sorry Honest Poet
Not today
Fuck it hey!

The one thing
That really kept me going
Made me keep my head high
My insides slightly glowing
A broken system
Had my emotions blowing

Final straw was a panic attack
The universe with a huge handed slap
Medication took over
Emotions take a nap

Losing my self worth
I've lost sight of self lack

Right now I'm living my worst hell
With no emotions to tell
Just wondering who the fuck I am
From this empty
Emotionless shell
Welcome to my kind of hell
No point in ringing the bell

No body home
You came for company
You'd be sitting alone
And all this from drip effect
Just an empty emotionless dome
Lights are on
Nobody's home

Drea MacMillan

On commitment

I choose mixed June blooms
A mass of scents, shapes, dew drenched
Let me touch them all

A lone stem soon bores
My nose tires of fading rose
Give me a bouquet

(#haikuchallenge)

Jon Collins

Perhaps, he thought
I ought
To give these mushrooms
The benefit
Of the doubt.

(#haikuchallenge)

Katherine Grace Hyslop

Playing

"Play away", that's what they used to say,
All day, any day, any-way!
Music with creativity, sandwiched together
(As they had been, really, since forever). But,
"Be Still now!" (and sedate).

Clip-Clop, Boom-Bam!
Softly marching 4/4 time.
Our musical-creations,
Boom! "Get in Line".

'Limited by public-regulations'.
We thought they'd never know, so
We crouched inside that Inner Sanctum.
Our tender years gave rise to courage
Which snapped!
After smiles were shared and
Her viola case fell-open, allowing a handgun to fall
Into that open-palm!
Pain filled my very being - beyond any words -
And a stench of iron, blasting-through,
As I sloshed about,
Rasping inanely, inside some warm-stickiness.
I was left. Still, thinking about 4/4 time,
While my mouth dried-out.

Carol Sheppard

Postcard
(With a nod to William Carlos Williams)

I'm sorry
I went
without you.

You said
you didn't
want to go.

I think
you would
have loved it
here.

Karlostheunhappy

Delighted to report that the following poem got 'Highly Commended' at the Dean Writers 2022 open poetry competition.
Not bad for a ditty sitting in a car park, waiting for the children at Cinderford cinema during a warm spring evening. It will be included in my next collection, which is coming along nicely.

PRAYER OF THE ZODIAC NIGHT 15TH APRIL 2022

evening
and only the soft treetops remain stroked by sun
(except for our Forest's now gold crown – May Hill);

even
a pale full Spring moon has risen early to regard her sweet golden
splendour
(whilst I scribble in a little notebook my full moon heart of loneliness) –

memories
like scars of scowles –
but this Aries evening

cares
not that torturing darkness
when, instead, the amber evening slumberlight slides to die and

slip
kindly into moonglow
(and thankfulness) –

This is actually a 'twin' poem, to be read as 4 stanzas, or as a short synthesis by the first word of each stanza, in a zen-like simplicity, like this…

evening
even memories
cares
slip

…I don't know if that's an established poetic form or not, but I worked it in that way. A couple of Forest of Dean points here; May Hill is our crowning glory – Robert Frost could see it from his cottage in Dymock (when it was the Muse Colony), but also appears in other Forest / Gloucestershire poets' work. The trees crown the peak and it's a very melancholy place to visit with panoramic views of neighbouring counties.

Scowles are cuts left in our landscape from iron ore works.

And on that evening, there was a pale moon up early as the sun was setting. Not one for zodiac astrology and wotnot this, then, was a challenge to come up with something on that theme whilst still staying true to my scepticism.

Nupur Chakrabarty

Rampage

This poem portrays the tumult of the present time, as the transcendental happenings blend with it. Nandi, the bull of Shiva seems angry storming over the world.

In the middle of the storm, alone
on the road life seems
barren, and none
appears for the waiting
eyes. True to life, and yet the surface loud,
the scene riotous now,
breakers on rampage.
The water, earth and wind creating a sudden fire of the thunders.
What bellows pierce through the gauze of the showers? An angry
Nandi runs rampant. A dance in the folds of time transpiring. Brilliant
feet of light caper over the upsurge.
From the zenith watching--
a froth of darkness whirring
in the abysmal gorge.

Tish Ince Poet

Real Bed

in my dreams I have a real bed
that I'm so damn proud of
that I'd read books in
eat overnight oats in
from Kilner Jars
in sunlit mornings
with bud vase lavender
on a tray with legs

in my dreams, I have purple silk
the nightdress that falls
split on my thigh
too cool when I first
slip it on
nipples pay attention
through the generous cup

in my dreams, sheets are taut
hair falling cool
in loose curls on pillows
or on the flat white
the overhead fan spins silently
keeping nipples erect in wait

in my dreams, his hand is hot
rests on my leg
moving slow, while he talks
of anything
anything
any damn thing
I've stopped listening

in this real bed
he is gone
in this real bed
dead, is his spot
this widow bed
like I almost forgot
like I almost forgot

Kuma san

Refugee

I cast myself to the wind,
loosed myself to freedom,
aimed for the horizon,
my vision bold
my heart brave
I trusted my dream

the promise of better,
the safety I sought,
the new world that would
open its splendour to me.

I can still see the horizon,
the dream I hold so dear
is closer than it's ever been.

Behind bars I am broken,
my dream does not want me!

Kuma x

Morgan (I'm not a Poet) Rye

Rule of Three
The Rule of Three is inspired by my first novel, Snowball Earth – Quinn.

She dreamed dreams,
And lay in abhorrent splendor
drugged by feeling
holding tight the rope of night
until morning drove it away.
And did not look upon herself,
for truth would show
in day lit mind.
Undeserving of ceremony
no witness congratulated
they came for her
the worst of human kind.
Fate told them
as once of darkness
of light,
and the balance of things.
But none, not one,
would dream as dark as she.
The Rule of Three could set it right
make her darkness light
Three did come,
a challenge: one,
to risk her life,
set balance right.
Came the crow and second; a foe
practiced in harm.
Revelation, and third a betrayal,
her life pillaged to bone.
Fate, Lord of might
Goddess of timeless sight
took who she was,
to make a stronger soul.

Battle weary, used and scarred,
endure she did
to pay her debt
and The Rule of Three wept.
Comforting lies lost power
when beginning met its end
entwined in shades of everything
dark light ever real
Nature is and always was
when tethered hearts in dream.
by Nature's hand of Fate and Rule
the Circle was complete.

Raine Geoghegan

SAINT SARAH THE PATRON SAINT OF THE ROMANI PEOPLE

Saint Sarah or Sara la Kali as she is also known is the patron saint of the Romani people. It is said that she was the servant of one of the three Mary's and she travelled by boat to the Camargue. Her statue remains in the shrine of Saint Marie de la Mer and every year she is carried down to the sea as part of a ritual which honours her and her close relationship to the Roma.

Her Names are Many
(A Reimagining of Sara-Kali, the Patron Saint of Gypsies)

Some call her 'blessed one', her names are many.

Look, there she goes,

dressed in her finery for a Gypsy Rommer.

Black leather boots, long purple dress,

gold around her neck and a feather in her hat.

She'll mingle with the guests,

drink wine until she's skimmished.

She'll hitch her skirts up and dance like the young ones.

Just before she leaves she'll give order and sing a song

that nobody knows but everyone loves

and then as if by magic,

she'll disappear into the shadows

into the dust that rolls along along

the empty streets and never settles.

Rommer: wedding; Skimmished – drunk.

Shrine at Sainte Marie de la Mer

Good Friday, 2020 - Lockdown

The shrine is empty today. No footfall except for one woman who comes daily to clean the statue of Sara-Kali. As she wipes the limbs of her beloved Saint, she sings, and the shrine is full with song. Once finished, she kneels, resting her bones.

'Sara-Kali is dreaming

a boat on the shore,

white horses galloping towards her,

she a young girl, wanting to do good.

The woman offers up her prayers, kisses the feet of her faithful Mother. Once she leaves, all is quiet and still, only the dark face in the corner of the room glistens in the final flicker of candlelight.

Lucky 'eather

She travels to Trafalgar Square, once a year, sits on the bench, feeds the pidgeons. She relives the old days, the market sellers. She sees it all now, vegetables, cheeses, nuts, the organ grinder and the barrow boys. There was one that they called Curly, on account of him having no hair. He would wink and smile at her, she a young girl calling out. 'lucky 'eather sir.'

The One

She is the one walking the long road/ the one stepping out of the rock/ the one being washed in the sea/ standing on the shore/ she opens her arms and the horses bow down their heads/ knowing her power.

Know My True Face

I'm a lot older than you think.

Look closely. See the dust in me eyes, the rivers in me veins.

Look at these 'ands, they carry the weight of the world yet never grow tired.

Man made me into a saint but my life belongs to my race and the days gone past,

a time when religion was found in the clay, in mountains and forests,

in the song of the wind and at a mother's breast.

The grains of truth 'ave scattered far but are found wherever we tread,

so keep 'movin', know that I am your mother, sister, midwife and the phuri dhai.

Come to me and know my true face.

(*Phuri dhai – the source of all Romany blood*)

Jason N Smith

S.A.D: Seasonal affective disorder

Coldness enfolds and darkness enshrouds,
in vacuum light diminishes this time of year.

Summer hides behind clouds, allows
Winter to walk in and talking turns to frost,
icy on ears.

Seasonal dark skies rain icy hail,
while wind breathes bleak breaths
over streets of minds and gas tokens
of life are too high a price,
too high a cost to buy.

And thoughts skate over mirror lakes
reflecting memories of heated haze of yesterday's,
and then race into distance mist of warm reveries,
that only hibernate.

Tish Ince Poet

Sewn on the bias

redress the inequality
this bias, binding her
She is not on the underskirt
of community

She is not some interface
between you and the
badly sewn fabric of society
where she is less

You have her tacked all wrong
lines on her skin are quilted
into hearts, she is softer
but made of firmer things

in this 'stitch up'
tailors in suits
seaming her in tight
bring a steaming outcry
from mouths no longer shut

patriarch her diagonally
intersection-ally
she struggled free
marched down catwalks
Anti-pirouette
those 'perfect 10' men?
become plus plus one
stronger on her own

ran homes, kids, shopping, business
countries and supreme courts
paid less - dressed for less

see her in the gown she has become
velveteen queen, mothers, sisters
men - break the bias
you have her sewn all wrong.

#BreakTheBias #poem #internationalwomensday #TishIncePoet

Louise Longson

Shroud

I am the nadir of stratification.
I have touched the earth.
It has made me unclean.
I am the untouchable,
tangible Dalit.

Beauty is for my elevated cousins; for them
the mystical mists, magical spindrift. They
are curls of angels' hair, the face of God.
I weave a dense carpet, threaded with envy.

I am the cold impenetrable slayer,
I will blind your vision, dim your lights.
I will come down on you suddenly, lethal.
I am the thin veil between prey and prayer.

Jason Conway

Silk

A feather glides
Gracefully stroking ether
A bridge between worlds

(#haikuchallenge)

Sue Hubbard

Silver Service

From 'Swimming to Albania', Salmon Poetry

Why should I suddenly remember,
after fifty years, that thirteen-year-old

crushed among the putrid hotel bins
behind the steamy kitchen door,

that meaty odour of gravy seeping
from his acned skin.

How little I knew as his wet tongue
slithered between my untutored lips,

his bitten fingers searched for the hooks
along my cotton schoolgirl bra.

I hardly knew whether the terror
of detection or the growing hardness

inside his waiter's trousers,
pressed against my yellow summer dress,

frightened me more. Was this love,
I wondered, as in the mirrored dining room

upstairs, the tuxedoed band played:
Fools Rush In,

while my parents waited
for Silver Service?

Derek Dohren

Skye

Remember me to Valtos
on the spume flecked road from Lealt
dinosaur bones and storm tossed
red zinc roofs over peat
to the rain drenched air of Storr
where the Trotternish rocks
descend down Staffin's shore
as gaelic gulls tumble and mock.

Remember me to Glasnakille
on the salt sprayed road from Elgol
to Sligachan and Kyleakin
and beaches of kelp and coral
to the mossy trek up Scorrybreac
atop the Portree brae
that wends from Shullishader Beag
and climbs above the bay.

Remember me.

Karlostheunhappy

Here's a quick senryu from me in 5-7-5...

snowdrop drink the sun
now it reaches the cold earth -
wakes like rising hope

(#haikuchallenge)

Adele Ogiér Jones

Snowdrops at imbolc
arrive with season's switching
recollecting Bride.

(#haikuchallenge)

Darcy Royce

Sorceress

You awaken in the depth of this old home,
soul,
like a cogent flame,
attracting peaceful valleys, and soundless mountain tops,
enchantress,
you fill my heart with love,
for this tiptoe vision,
for another's sacred essence,
encased in a message bearing dove.

I know if anyone, you possess the ascertain breadth,
to call for and receive him within,
serenity in flight..
this halcyon lover of mine,
show him my unpolluted sea,
walk with him
on my golden shores,
lay down with him - give yourself again,
to irenic, sweet, encores.

M. Palowski Moore (Silver Lion Poet)

SPIRIT DANCERS

Swaying back and forth
They move like wind
Through flickering leaves
Of ancient trees.
Both young and old summon
Ancestral lights; healing energy
Of reflection, heritage, community.

Through a crystalline sky
Blazed blue, white, gold
Blessed wings glide, sail
Through soulful air
Float in streams of rainbows
While gilded ghosts
Whirl, twirl; sacred tops spinning
Dancers dazzling
Among mists and mountain ash.

Shadows converge, emerge
Entice, invite us
To remember authentic movements;
Motions that celebrate
Expression, passion, unity
Remind us to rise and raise up
To always dance as if
Our lives were on fire.

M. Palowski Moore, SLP

Agu Chinedu Ejorh

STANDING OVATION FOR THE WOMAN

This poem was originally chosen for The Trawler 2021. However due to illness we were unable to get permission to include it. We are happy to say that we now have permission and it takes its place in this edition.

We are many and unannounced.
Beautiful, wonderful creation.
Raising kings, building the nation.
Weaning armies with our hugs and kisses.
Bearing in our hands, our hearts broken into pieces.

We are many and unsaluted
Violent natural catalytic ions.
Lionesses behind the great lions.
Fed kings with nourishment from our chests.
Bearing on our bodies, our scars as crests.

We are many and unnoticed.
Finest golds, glittering.
Skylights of pearls, flickering.
Filling the earth from our wombs.
Bearing in our hearts, our memories as wounds.

We are many and unappreciated.
Mysterious powerful goddesses.
Keepers of kins' fortresses.
Masterminded victories with our few suggestions.
Bearing in our souls, our burden of oppressions.

They are many and should be celebrated.
Angel personified, woman.
Help fit for man.
Considered unequal to Adam.
But a lot more than him to complete him.

Matty Blades

star burst haiku

Each star meets its burst
Sending shards across the void
Spawning other worlds

(#haikuchallenge)

Karlostheunhappy

STARS KEEP VIGIL
Read at February's Crafty Crows, the monthly GPS open mic

Stars keep vigil over your sleep –

      How softly the night arrives when I am with you,
except when the moaning clouds forgather & helpless walls rise raw &
tall –

Then, perhaps, I will step back into the velvet universe,
      slip into the neon waves, drown in the dust of stars,
slide there in my own open resting –

      Nature and all its beauty are nothing,
      nothing more than the oblivion of creation rejoicing,
      rejoicing in its magical nothing & everything everness –

Anyway, and after all, the universe sent me
      so she has every right to claim me, especially when I am empty
empty darkdowndead in the gloom as dead
      as the glorious entropy from whence I came –

Then, when I am gone, you will know that her stars watch over you
still –
      At least that it is what I hope –
That hope   my deepest hope   you could call 'love' –

Sue Finch

Swinging

The swing has picked up the rhythm of my body and I am head back smiling. I was always other, I say as my feet stretch out in front of me. When I was little, the staccato beginnings of back and to and that juddering pull of the chain links before they found their rhythm felt wrong. I always wanted someone to push me. And before I even sat down back then I would imagine biting the seat because to me it was a newly unwrapped strawberry fruit sweet. Now I like the work of it before the freedom of shoes against clouds. I swear one day my soles will touch the sky.

Sue Finch

The Coin

I imagine putting that pound coin in my mouth
tonguing it from heads to tails
and back again.
A clock somewhere struck eight
as you walked in
while the minute hand of the one I was eyeing
clicked its thirtieth tick.
Your hair
your skirt
your make-up
your eyes straight ahead
told me
I was out of your league.
Then that fumble of fingers
had the coin falling from your grip.
Just one flaw was all I needed to say my name.
Like a one-armed bandit on triple seven
I rattled out the stories of my life
and still you said yes to a coffee I wouldn't make
and paused on the bridge over the canal
to kiss me.
I could love that pound coin forever
take its metallic tang again and again.

Ivor Daniel.
Posting this on the anniversary of Lennon's death. RIP John.

the day ahead of me

dis com bob ul at ed
out of sorts
incomprehensiblequicksandthoughts
the day ahead of me
trips
up
that very moment when I see
News headline sign in front of me

Lennon
Shot

Jon Collins

The doorway in my mind is a metaphor

The long street that winds, and vanishes
Into the mist, a question still unanswered
From childhood, but before, inherent to my nature
The staircase that leads into the unknown
To places as yet unshown, but more than that
Pathways in between, connections unattainable
Stone balconies above, leading from and to
Their sources accessible
Only to the acolytes of some unfathomable religion
As much architectural as tangible,
Like in a vast cathedral,
But that, too, is metaphorical
The covered steps leading down
Into the unbegotten recesses of my consciousness
Missing links, ladders and snaking passageways
As yet, unmapped , their purpose untapped
Fragile ceilings, in places collapsed
And all this to say
Perhaps there is a way, from here to wherever
But equally, maybe, its very inaccessibility
Was the point of the similarity
That ancient corridor, forever under lock and key
Never to be reached, at least, not by me.

Louise Longson
A haiku (western 5-7-5) inspired by sitting in my garden tonight.

The jasmine flowers
Like stars fallen from the sky
Scattered in your hair

(#haikuchallenge)

Darcy Royce

"Music, when soft voices die,
Vibrates in the memory—
Odours, when sweet violets sicken,
Live within the sense they quicken."
                    ... Percy Shelley

The Mellowing

Like dew that lifted from the flowers,
at the break of velvet dawns,
and, in rising,
gave its last breath - like
bluebirds,
earthly anchors,
departed,
now lost to the horizon,
infinite, or so I thought,
like a melody - you sang to me,
stuck and rusting in a belle epoque gramophone,
dust settling on remembrance,
like a sweet abandon,
lovers feel in each other's arms,
after the last breath,
and a brand-new one's birth,
like the last message,
written in invisible ink, never sent,
never read,
pointless,
I am at peace with this mellowing,
all is -
forgiven, forgotten, gone.

Charlie Markwick

The Olive Tree

Sunday quiet, just a host of birds,
and old church bell striking four.
No Spanish chatter nor children
playing and calling in the air.

The sun warms this spot on village square
just me and this squat and ancient olive tree.
I'm glad it cannot talk as this allows imagination
the romantic sort to muse on what it's seen.

No doubt the truth has much more
grit and dark, things that would mar
the good nature in my heart, brought
on by this early springing glow.

I wonder if this tree will mark this time.
Me beside on wooden bench; breaking off
my journey back to France.
It may not, but I shall store
away this precious tranquil hour.

Cubillas de Santa Marta 06/02/22

Jason Conway

There are no more tears;
no more hopeful smiles,
only the labour
of my sighs,
for the frightbringer
infects my sleep
with chilled sweat
and grief
and all is drained from me
into the abyss.
I am numb;
A winter mist.
What good will come of this?
What light can come
when the wallow
blocks the sun?
I wait here petrified
in need of love,
longing for the thaw
and my rise.

When my heart comes back to life.

Clive Oseman.

THE REAL THING

It was irony on a scale to make Alanis blush.
The final of the slam
and the last performer slayed it
with a passion that would have crushed
the strongest opposition.

She knew she had clinched the top position
with a tirade against capitalism
so fierce as to make the Tories fear prison,
put Labour's rightward drift into remission
and put Corbyn to the right
of the new world order.

The scores came in. Five perfect tens
and watching promoters
doubted they could afford her
now the media were sure to laud her
and she would be recognised across all borders.

The audience of twenty-nine
clubbed together for a bottle of wine
but she refused it
was offered Pepsi but eschewed it
and took a glass of water from the tap.

That's right. The tap..
Oh crap

Soon it was all over Facebook,
number one trending on insta and Twitter
and Evian shares went down the shitter.
Perrier did a similar thing
and Buxton Spring was no longer a thing.

And here's the sting.

Cristiano Ronaldo,
the worlds second best soccer bloke
who wiped 4 billion dollars
off the value of coke
was again second fiddle-
and this is no joke-
To a teenage slammer from the city of Stoke..

Jon Collins

There's something to be said

There's something to be said
About burying your head
Playing on while Rome burns
Blinking at catastrophe
Weaving Armageddon
Into life's more superficial twists and turns
And so, you walk among the dead
Traipse the virtual mortuary
Distant voyeurism into another's plight
Albeit that the chasm filled with faraway despair
Isn't quite aligned with your line of sight
Disaster unfolds, directed by remote control
Split-screens onto screams
Detached, you latch onto a face
Fleetingly steering near embrace
Of where once was a soul
A momentary pause as you so nearly
Touch the shattered peace of another
Then it too disintegrates
Fragments, pieces
Lost in the maelstrom of tickers and head noise
Weak against the bleak
Attracted by distraction
The moment for empathy is gone
Life makes its way, beyond
The anguish of elsewhere
And you
Have already
Moved on

Louise Diamant

The traveler

I have packed my
frustration and my anger
and left both behind me
While I ride on the back
of giants
on roads
less travelled
Listening to my heartbeat
and the wind in naked
branches
My companion walks with
heavy force and checks
to see if the luggage I
so eagerly demand to carry
is safely stored a thousand miles
behind us
I let my head drop and
cry tears of frustration and
anger into his
Not all emotions are meant to be
packed and left behind
Some are carried on the back
of giants on roads less travelled.

Morgan (I'm not a Poet) Rye

The vlogger, the baker, the mortgage maker.

She just set up an online bakery,
now she has a gun
He helped us fill out forms at the bank,
now he's holding a gun

The Russians may not come at all
But are not so far away
Protesters are locked behind bars
or worse
most look the other way

There was no time for the vlogger to be afraid
when the shell hit
later that evening, he drank a little vodka
smoked a cigarette
and the shaking started.

Morgan I'm-not-a-poet Rye

Trevor Valentine

Timber Cries

Timber!!
Cries the crashing world
Falling upon the crocodile eyes
Poking from underneath the shoreline
Its eternity unfettered
Its timeline content to wait
Sits quietly
Until we
Are all
Gone

From choke filled ashes
Only the mythical Phoenix will survive
See, oh, too, the blanket
Smothering your cold
Soon inert breath

Yet, saunter on
Into your own discreet doom
No gloom
For walking backwards
You only see the footprints behind you
Not the once iced cliff in front

Timber cries
In ignorance and darkness
The shoreline grows
White horse stallions
Stand ready
To clutch
To snatch
To reap
To scythe
Grimly

Julian Roger Horsfield

To Cheer Up Digger Down

Interwoven within the hedge
a robin's nest, and just besides
there runs a gentle flowing river.
The sun upon the wheat is gold,
the cider sweet and strong
and there's time for another.

Along the lines are perching
swifts that graceful haunt
my waking thoughts, And by
the path beside the field edge
just beyond the drystone wall
a badger city.

Perhaps we'll go there for
the love of all, and in the
evening of the day,
crouch down, and quiet
wait for come what may.

Here comes a sow, dragging
her fresh new grassy bed!
Unfazed by us, short-sighted
as they are, they cannot sniff
us in the breeze!

Our hearts grow deeper
in badger love, and then
out comes a badger cub and
not long after half a dozen more!
And my father with a torch that's
shining in the boughs we see
through the darkness clearly.

They stick around for peanuts
spread about, and the barn owl
up top flits through the beam
hunting for a shrew or mouse,
all white her plumes, an angel
from a lofty perch, calls aloft,
her proud visage, her sharp beak
and claws, her bluey marbled
spots and hues of gold and
white and silver grey
what lover could deny.

And through the moonlit woods come
fallow deer with senses sharp,
and spotted white upon their rich and
seemly rumps, the stag majestic oversees
with antlers formed and prodding proud,
too soon to rut, keeps pace about
the does and peace amongst
the fast maturing bucks.

And you and I by moonlight ride
on double-painted bikes with
whirring lamps go softly back
full of joy along the Lower Meand
to join the Cinder Hill.

The hour is past ten, the weather close,
these hours the glowing fiery tips of
Gloucester life, a deep abiding
paradise though we knew not how
rare such pursuit, nor what
our fortune yet to be,
In the freedom fields of green
to gather 'shrooms, and count
the eggs, and catch the
trout ~ I see them yet ~

in the tumbling brook
that gushed on through
the Hudnall's wood
brown and flexing in
the bubbling pools.

Those days ~ were they so
different now that time
has rearranged?
All our innocence corrupted
with the mess? For I can walk
the self-same place, and
overcome the fence
and still in all there's brock.

The timeless brock who
shoulders digging,
and breeds in nursery
suites, whose home
extends so far and wide
he's safe assured
through winter's chilly night.
Tell me this is not alive!

Scott Cowley *(aka Rusty Goàt the Poet)*

Vomit

I climbed the highest tree to be found
and from the top I witnessed the three hundred and sixty degrees of
desolation abound

the panoramic history laid bare upon it
the scorched cracked bleeding earth
the pieces of my heart broken and fragmented
shattered with the violence of a hammer

all those memories so vivid laying shrivelled
dry cracked weeping open sores
each why and why not
each opportunity squandered and lost
each step that I should never had trod
bearing down upon me like a martyr bears a cross

twisted up by decades of mental chains
twisted up by the rotting carcass of what remains
twisted up by the screaming inside my brain
twisted rotting searing black decay

I climbed the highest tree to be found
and from the top I witnessed myself jump from it
screaming into the never ending black hole of life's vomit

M. Palowski Moore (Silver Lion Poet)

WAITING

It's 3AM
And I am waiting
Waiting for you
A spark of inspiration
To ignite a new passion
A new journey
To believe in.
Alone
My compositions
Are folly
My music
Is pedestrian
The songs
Are vague and soulless.
The whiskey
Does not keep promises.
It is nothing
More than distraction.
The piano waits
For my affectionate touch
The caress
Of excitement
To bring life again
And I am standing
Waiting
While the world
Sleeps and wanders in dreams.

M. Palowski Moore, SLP

Scott Cowley *(aka Rusty Goàt the Poet)*
(notes from a hospital bed/observations/180921)

waiting waiting waiting...

canulated wrist
green patterned pyjamas
brown toast for breakfast

drugs trolley
four hourly obs
constant ECG monitoring
bland sandwiches for lunch

waiting...

adjustable hospital bed
vinyl upholstered chair, blue
hand wash basin
tap water not for consumption

this hospital
has become
my universe

on a waiting list
to have my chest
ripped open

canulated wrist
four hourly obs
adjustable hospital bed

waiting waiting waiting...

hand wash basin
tiger striped bag
offensive waste for incineration

a selection of differing sized latex free gloves
for examinations

waiting for a transfer
chest ripped open
surgical procedure

brown toast for breakfast
sandwiches for lunch
hand wash basin
waiting…

nurses station
vinyl upholstered chair
nurses station
vinyl upholstered chair
repetition
repetition
repetition

notice board
polite reminders
acute cardiac unit ward routine
new staff rotation

waiting
four hourly observations
waiting for chest to be ripped open

waiting…

Sally Aspden

Walking Meditation

In a soft swirl of misty stars
our world is turning. Here you stand.
Let heart rest easy. You belong.

Knowing you're as important
as any other, that your next footfall
is all you need to do right now,

place your foot slowly, gently
into your next step.

I can't give you security.
But know this: the most important thing
in the furthest reach of space and time
among misty stars in a clear-black night
and the busiest rooms of their hectic towns -

- the most important thing -
is your quiet turn of heel and toe,
soft touch of foot with ground.

Charlie Markwick
Note to readers. In Thai the stress is on the first syllable of Kamala, like camera.

Weals

I've never driven on a bike before
at least not the sort that purrs and growls.
These last two days I've rectified that lack.

Up and down the hills to Kamala we went
twisting, turning with the windy road.
Chicanery abounds and leaning into every bend
plucks the thrilling chords inside my head.

The fear of hurt is never far away. So close
to the gritty surface I'm speeding on.
But that exposure brings opulence as well.
Rich sounds and smells that are hidden in a car,
birdsong, dogs and unbelievably the sea.

Smell of wood smoke richens up the air,
the scent of flowers,
incense in the roadside shrines.
And passing massage parlours a hint of oils
sneak through the rushing air.

But everything has a price to pay.
Despite the tiny footprint of the bike
a U turn seems to take such space.

And off I come. Asphalt snatches at my skin,
kerb attacks my shoulder blade. My new red
shorts, comfy, a subtle burgundy;
ripped and stained with claret blood
bright against my legs. And such is life
no broken bones but a twisted ego and a bike.

Patong 11/12/21

Carol Sheppard   5

woken from the dead
earth by spring's piercing warmth
the snowdrops appear

(#haikuchallenge)

Marilyn Timms

Words that cannot be
unsaid. Doors slammed. Car leaving.
Pillow full of tears.

(#haikuchallenge)

Adele Ogiér Jones

woven to match snow
drops, first past winter solstice
bursting through late snow

(#haikuchallenge)

The Poets

Adele Ogiér Jones

41   **Collected walnuts**   *(#haikuchallenge)*
53   **Foraging last days**   *(#haikuchallenge)*
119   **Snowdrops at Imbolc**   *(#haikuchallenge)*
150   **woven to match snow**   *(#haikuchallenge)*

Adèle Ogiér Jones is a member of The Poetry Society (UK). She is published in anthologies and online poetry journals, with a trilogy of 72 poems on art of Swiss artist Anni Zindel by Picaro Poets (2021), and a new collection of poems on Irish rivers, Following Rivers in Trees (Ginninderra Press, 2022). Sixteen of her tanka-form poems appear in Poetry for the Planet (Litoria Press, Australia, 2021) as 'Lost Love Song' and 'Tanka for the Planet'.

Agu Chinedu Ejorh

122   STANDING OVATION FOR THE WOMAN

He is from Ghana, his style of writing, his swift manipulation of words and his ability to use anything to communicate makes him an outstanding writer. He is the evolution of the modern African poetry.

His book, 'Echoes Of Africa' by Chinedu Ejorh, was published in 2008 by Trafford.

Akondo Nouhe-Dine

62   **Heaviness**

Nouhr-Dine D. Akondo writes drama and poetry both in French and English. Senior Lecturer of his home university, he lives in Lomé the capital city of Togo, West Africa. He is a co-organiser of the "Festival International des Lettres et Arts" (FESTILARTS) at the University of Lomé. He writes and draws much of his subject matter from African culture and history and is interested in Contemporary World socio-economic and political issues.

His poems have been published in a number of African poetry magazines, namely Afro-poésie (Online), Best New African Poetry 2016, Contemporary Poetry from Africa (2019), COVID-19 DIARY: World's Anthology of Poetry (2020), I Can't Breathe: A Poetic Anthology of Fresh Air (2020).

Amy Bingham

51   **evening**   *(#haikuchallenge)*

Originally from South Gloucestershire, Amy Bingham has always immersed herself in writing and the spoken word, first as a Broadcast Journalist and News Editor, and then as a Local Government Communications Manager. However, in 2016, she decided to follow her passion for animal welfare and left her position to work for a leading animal charity.

It was only recently (since the pandemic) that she picked up her trusted pen and notepad and rediscovered the joy of writing poetry - with her family, four-legged friends and the North Devon landscape, where she now lives, being her main inspiration.

Website: amybinghampoetry.weebly.com/
Twitter: @amybingham

Ann D Stevenson

21   A Passing Storm

Ann is retired and living in Gloucestershire, UK. She has had a few poems published, under the name of Ann D Stevenson, not to be confused with that well known poet, Anne Stevenson.

Ann-Marie Kurylak

48   DON'T BREAK DOWN

Ann-Marie Kurylak would describe herself as a poet of the heart as her work stems from raw emotion. Originally from Gloucester in England, she now lives in Tilburg in the Netherlands with her Dutch partner and spends her free time exploring her Dutch home and learning the language.

Carol Sheppard

50   Evening   (*#haikuchallenge*)
78   In case of emergency
99   Postcard
148   woken from the dead   (*#haikuchallenge*)

Carol Sheppard is a poet and playwright who lives in the beautiful Forest of Dean, which inspires much of her poetry. She has been published in several poetry journals and her poems have been exhibited in the Biggar Poetry Garden. She is an active member of several local writing groups and has started taking part in open mic events to share her poetry with others.

Charlie Markwick

29   Behind The North Wind
131   The Olive Tree
147   Weals

Charlie Markwick is a Gloucestershire born spoken word performer, poet and storyteller. He grew up in the Cotswolds and now lives in the Haute-Pyrénées. A long time GPS member, Charlie was for a period, poet in residence at Gloucester Library. In 2019 he published his first pamphlet of poems "Orienteering", pieces from his show of the same name. He has been included in the GPS Anthologies: "Magic" (2019), and "The Trawler" (2020 and 2021). Also in "Today I feel Hawaii" (2019) edited by the then Gloucestershire Poet Laureate Brenda Read-Brown. Two poems were published on Good Dadhood (https://gooddadhood.com/2020/05/24/two-poems-by-charlie-markwick/). His poems about dementia have been included in resources created by the NHS. In 2020 Bream Community Library produced videos of him reading his work for their Poetry Box Project (https://www.breamcommunitylibrary.co.uk/charlie-markwick-2). Charlie is still working with musicians and visual artists around the world on a project combining their compositions and his words.

Chloë Jacquet

23   AT THE AIRPORT

Chloë Jacquet is a multicultural, multifaceted spoken word artist based in Gloucestershire. She was 2017 Oxford Hammer & Tongue slam champion and twice reached the semi-finals of the National Slam Finals at the Royal Albert Hall.

With a preference for straight talking and a penchant for rhymes and opinions, Chloë's poetry is both entertaining and meaningful. Her work deals with a wide variety of subjects, ranging from workplace discrimination and mental health, to the pressures placed on modern men, via her short-term relationship with a biscuit.

Chloë thinks name dropping is really uncool. As well as her own headline slots, she has supported artists such as Elvis McGonagall, Joelle Taylor and Hollie McNish and her work has featured several times on the BBC.

Her first collection Take It By The Line is published by Black Eyes Publishing UK.

Chloë can be found on social media using the handle @ChloeJPoetry.

Clive Oseman

133   THE REAL THING

Clive Oseman is a Swindon based Brummie multi slam-winning spoken word artist, comedian, satirist and promoter who is now headlining events internationally in the real world as well as online with his blend of the satirical, the surreal and the slightly absurd. He regularly teams up with Nick Lovell to host events, usually under the Oooh Beehive banner. His third poetry collection It Could be Verse was published by Black Eyes Publishing in 2020. His debut one-man show "What if they laugh at me?" debuted in Birmingham on May 8th.

Dane Ince

74   **Imagination: Text**

Dane Ince traveled from his place of birth in Texas to Berkeley, California to study art. His work is concern with place-where the artist comes from and their journey and how the fine art expression shapes itself into a journalistic expression. William S. Burroughs and South American writer Jorge Luis Borges are some of his favorites. He is on the Beat-dada spectrum between Marcel Duchamp and Andrew Goldsworthy. Recently tapped by the National Beat Poetry Foundation to be the Beat Poetry Laureate for California 2022-2024. Published internationally, and host of a weekly open mis zoom program.

Darcey Royce

49   **Electrical Wire**
120   **Sorceress**
130   **The Mellowing**

Darcy Royce is a poet from the county of Wiltshire in the UK. She writes about the human condition and self in its many facets, with the intention to model how poetry can be a powerful means to heal through creative writing.

As a clinical hypno-CBT therapist and coach, Darcy combines therapeutical elements with the creative process itself to bring about breakthrough and recovery from trauma.

Derek Dohren

45   **Diana and Dai**
92   **My Mate Steve**
117   **Skye**

The avatar masquerading as Derek Dohren was manufactured in Liverpool but has received countless upgrades, modifications and downgrades in Scotland, Spain and more latterly, the south-west of England. It continues to be moulded, shaped, fattened up, diseased, cut, bumped, abused, and occasionally loved and/or hated. For the most part though it has been considered by fellow avatars to be a total irrelevance. As its overworked atoms trundle its path towards the inevitable day of recycling, it knocks out what has laughingly been described by some as 'poetry', while remaining determinedly fixed on the quest for the perfect cup of tea.

Derek's two poetry collections, 'Everything Rhymes with Orange' ISBN-13 978-1913195038 and 'Wasp in My Cockpit' ISBN-13 978-1913195137 (Black Eyes Publishing UK), are a celebration of a unique style, described by one astute commentator as 'quietly subversive'.

Devlin Wilson

47   **DISCO DOGS**

Devlin Wilson lives and works in Gloucester and is a long-time member of the GPS.

Doreen Baidoo

69   Hunting

I was conceived in Jamaica, born in London and, from the ages of 17-34years, was married to a Ghanaian.

During my life I have lived in Jamaica, Ghana and half way up a mountain in Corsica, each for a couple of years.

London had always been my base until I returned from Corsica, then for the next 20years I lived in Bristol which is where I started to acknowledge the poet within myself.

Encouraged by The Bristol Black Writers Group I began performing my poetry with my work being published in some anthologies.

I retired to the Gloucestershire countryside to write - but didn't for 5 years, instead I spent my time gadding about being a happy OAP! During the 1st Corona lockdown, I started to knit sweaters, which has continued with a vengeance that, even I, cannot believe.

Now writing and knitting compete for my time.

Drea MacMillan

17   **A Circle of Bone**   *(#haikuchallenge)*
24   **Avebury: The Outer Circle**
96   **On commitment**   *(#haikuchallenge)*

Andrea Macmillan lives in the quaint town of Malmesbury in Wiltshire with her ever faithful rescue dog Jack. She has always loved writing and began her first novel at the tender age of seven after being inspired by Enid Blyton's 'The Wishing Chair'. She is a passionate reader and has an eclectic taste in books from the classics to modern African American literature. Her ideal way to spend the day is by the beach with her nose in a book. Her love of reading and writing paved the way to her career as a copywriter and she now runs her own business, Drea Macmillan Social Marketing.

Her earlier work focuses on her experience as a domestic violence survivor. Nature and her love of travel feature strongly in her more recent work which explore the themes of lust, love and loss.

A powerful performance poet, Drea has headlined at several poetry events in Cheltenham, Swindon and Gloucester.
IG @drea.macmillan
Facebook @dreamacmillan
www.dreamacmillan.com

Elvis Gregory-Sayce

80   **Insomnia**

83   **{ It's All About U }**   *(#haikuchallenge)*

My3VerZ

I was first introduced to creative writing at Age 8 at my Junior school by a Creative teacher
In 1972.

One day as an exercise he placed a Red Candle on the table and said write what you see.

I wrote 4 Stanzas
Without even knowing I did it,
Which surprised the teacher and told me I had wrote a Poem.

It was featured in the school magazine and praised by other teachers. When they asked me what I wrote about, I said life, whereas the other kids wrote about, a Red Candle, they said I had used the candle as a metaphor.

It inspired me to carry on Writing

Currently working on a Poetry Book Project, I have been creating this over the last 2 years, at some point it will be finished.

Henry Farrell

39   **CLOAK THE DAY IN DUSK**

Heavenly Blessing.

Ivor Daniel

20   **another moon haiku**   (*#haikuchallenge*)
31   **Bonfire '21**   (*#haikuchallenge*)
127   **the day ahead of me**

Ivor's poems have appeared in A Spray of Hope, wildfire words, Steel Jackdaw, Writeresque, iamb~wave seven, Fevers of the Mind, The Trawler 2021, Roi Fainéant, Ice Floe Press, The Dawntreader, After..., Alien Buddha, Block Party, Black Nore Review, Orchard Lea Anthology (Cancer) 2022, and Crump's Barn Anthology (Halloween) 2022.

@IvorDaniel

Jason Conway

16   **A Celtic Dream**   (*#haikuchallenge*)
36   **Cerberus Smited**
70   **I fall weightlessly**   (*#haikuchallenge*)
79   **Inhale**   (*#haikuchallenge*)
115   **Silk**   (*#haikuchallenge*)
132   **There are no more tears**

Jason Conway is a professional daydreamer, based in Stroud, Gloucestershire, drawing inspiration from mental health and the transformative power of nature. He is a Co-Director of the Gloucestershire Poetry Society, and founder and editor of indie arts magazine Steel Jackdaw. Jason is published in Poetry Undressed, The Blue Nib, Poetry Bus, The Poetry Village and Impspired magazines. He has an MA in Creative Writing from Bath Spa University. Jason is an Arts Council funded poet, commissioned for the 2022 Stoke-on-Trent Umbrella Project.

www.thedaydreamacademy.com
www.steeljackdaw.com

Jason N Smith

111   S.A.D: Seasonal affective disorder

Jason N Smith is an award winning writer and spoken word artist and has read at Roundhouse, Royal Festival Hall, Tate Modern, National Theatre, The St Ethelburga's Centre for Reconciliation and Peace, New Vic and various festivals and events nationally. He has been involved in BBC Listener Project, National Prison Radio at BBC Broadcasting House and opened HMPPS National Care Experienced Peoples Conference at Leicester Race Course.

Jason has read at London's Literature Festival and launched Koestler Arts anthology after judging the spoken word category awards and features in the anthology with his platinum award poem: 'Stop and research.' Jason has published a popular collection of poetry titled: Beyond Words and has also released an album and book titled: The Word with 'I Witness band.' Jason is a trustee of SafeGround, a criminal justice arts charity addressing criminal justice matters with drama and programmes. Jason has worked as a Community Support Worker for CRC Probation and is a development coach for young people in care.

Jon Collins

97   **Perhaps, he thought**
128   **The doorway in my mind is a metaphor**
135   **There's something to be said**

Jon is a writer based in Brimscombe, Gloucestershire. He is the author of several music and technology-related books, and has far too many projects on the go — right now a fantasy novel, a musical and a fictionalised account of Paganini's life and work. He might even finish them one day.

You can find him at www.joncollins.info, on Twitter @jonno or Facebook www.facebook.com/thejoncollinspage

Josephine Lay

13   Anthology
22   A single last star   (*#haikuchallenge*)

Josephine Lay is a poet and author living between Gloucester and Cheltenham. She has a jnt. BA(Hons) in Creative Studies in Eng. & English Lit. and an MA in Creative Writing from Bath Spa University.

During 2018 Josephine suffered two falls, both resulting in concussion and a period of post-concussion syndrome. This precipitated Josephine into writing poetry and she joined The Gloucestershire Poetry Society (GPS). She became host of 'Squawkers' – a monthly poetry event in Cheltenham and since the Pandemic, Josephine hosts the online Zoom event, 'Crafty Crows', which has become highly successful and International. In Jan 2020 Josephine became Director of Operations for the GPS.

Josephine's most recent poetry collection is entitled A Quietus (2021). Her previous collections, Unravelling (2019) and Inside Reality (2018), all published by 'Black Eyes', and available from Amazon and to order from your usual bookseller throughout the world. For signed copies, go to the 'Black Eyes Shop…

https://www.blackeyespublishinguk.co.uk/shop
https://www.blackeyespublishinguk.co.uk/josephine-lay-poet

Julian Roger Horsfield

139   To Cheer Up Digger Down

Karlostheunhappy

28   **Basho and Buddha**   (*#haikuchallenge*)
91   **Moon**   (*#haikuchallenge*)
100   **PRAYER OF THE ZODIAC NIGHT 15TH APRIL 2022**
118   **snowdrop drink the sun**   (*#haikuchallenge*)
124   **STARS KEEP VIGIL**

In, 2022 Karlostheunhappy was awarded the title of Beat Poet Laureate (England) 2022/23 by the National Beat Poetry Foundation, inc. (USA); was 2021 Ledbury Poetry Festival 19th Slam runner-up and his work has featured in Beatdom, Steel Jackdaw and BeatSurreal.

A member of Gloucestershire Poetry Society and Dean Writers Circle, his collection of his first 30 years of writing was released in 2021 as 'OBLIVION: 200 Seasons of Pain & Magic' through his Gloomy for Pleasure imprint, available through Amazon.co.uk or .com – follow him on Facebook.com/karlostheunhappy

Katherine Grace Hyslop

98   **Playing**

Katherine Grace Hyslop: Born in glorious Filey, Yorkshire, I wandered around England. In 2000 I settled in Stroud with my amazing 'children'. Since before I started school, I have been writing the occasional poem; those very early poems were prayer-like.

I have enjoyed Creative Writing Workshops periodically; and more recently have been a member of the Gloucestershire Poetry Society, which, to my mind is usually a fun and enriching experience. I have some minor (esoteric) publications in the field of Health Promotion/Public Health.

I play the piano, and sometimes I compose a melody; most likely inspired by a person I care about or an unusual event, for example.

Kelly Owen

66   Homeless
94   No body's home

Born with a different name, changed when I decided to walk away from a past of destructive abuse, for many years I blamed myself, I believed that all those things imbedded into my brain as a child were actually true.

I've led a colourful life, no regrets, you can't change the past, but I can take those lessons to shape my future away from the person I don't want to be, towards nourishing the real me.

In 2008, I stumbled in to poetry, writing my first ever poem 'The dreaded eviction'. I was six months shy of twenty-four, ten minutes later producing my second 'A voice of its own!' which is a quite well known and loved, and the only one I have written that is fiction, the rest are my personal diary, my life!

My emotional damage has affected me so much, I looked scary to a lot of people as I wore a solid brick wall. In November 2020 this came crashing down, I was introduced to network marketing and many inspirational people I now call friends. This was the start of an amazing adventure, still coming with its ups and downs but moving forward. A good friend introduced me to my current company, I am The Honest Poet, and an Independent Consultant in nutrition, as well as a few more things I'm building alongside them.

I'm on a mission of self-discovery while trying to fund bringing nutrition to the homeless out of my own pocket. I WILL MAKE THIS HAPPEN!!!

Come find me;
https://www.facebook.com/kelly.owen.35912
https://www.facebook.com/groups/628870297524588/?ref=share_group_link
Kelly.owen.35912 - Instagram account
@kellyowen1985 - TikTok

Kezzabelle Ambler

71   Ignorance Abyss

Bard of Northampton, published performance poet, Kezzabelle Ambler, playfully weaves her wit and wisdom, expressing and connecting through her shows and 'Weaving Words' creative writing workshops around the country.

Her fifth book 'Permission To Speak' is full of mischief, observation of nature, green issues, mental health, racism, love, faith and hope She performs and works in the community, festivals & mental health wards helping people to express their thoughts, feelings, giving a voice for their story so their pen can be a tool for life.

She tours the country sharing her adventures baring all in her craft aiming to bless and encourage whoever crosses her path. She exudes passion and energy, her love of people and words is boundless. www.kezzabelle.co.uk.

https://www.facebook.com/kezzabelle.poet
Https://www.instagram.com/kezzabelleambler
https://Twitter.com/KezzabellePoet
Kezzabelle Ambler YouTube Channel,
                        https://www.youtube.com/KezzabelleAmbler
Linked In, https://www.linkedin.com/in/kezzabelle-ambler-56302023
TikTok@kezzabelleambler, https://vm.tiktok.com/ZMRA4GMGo/

Kuma San

61   Half the sky
87   Ittai
105   Refugee

Kuma San lives a few miles outside Gloucester. She is a novice, lay Buddhist priest and currently runs popular, weekly online meditation sessions, using a collection of resonating instruments. Kuma is an instinctive composer, percussionist and musician, playing singing bowls, large gong and cymbals as well as rainmakers, sticks and mouth sounds to create a deeply moving, meditative experience.

Recently Kuma has turned her creativity towards words. Her poetry echoes her music and speaks of her joy of nature, her gentleness and compassion for all beings. She's become an active member of the local poetry scene, and took part in the GPS 'Raised Voices' celebration of 'International Women's Day' at St Mary de Crypt, Gloucester, in February 2020. The poem she read on that day, 'Forget Me Not 2', is in The Trawler 2020.

Lou Hotchkiss-Knives

52   First Day Back

Born in Northern France, Lou Hotchkiss-Knives is a teacher, punk singer/songwriter and occultist living in Devon.

Her short stories are published by Veneficia Publications (https://www.veneficiapublications.com/) in the anthologies " 22 Tales from the Tarot", "So... Do We Have a Deal ?" and "Voices from the ashes".

She has also contributed to the poetry anthology "songs of the black flame" available on Black Moon Publishing. : https://www.blackmoonpublishing.com/

Louise Diamant

136   The traveler

Louise W Diamant. Born in 1975 in Denmark. Poet. Speaker. Stage performer in her one-woman show, at poetry slams and other poetry events. Published her first poetry collection in English in 2021 called Word Warrior Woman – Power through poetry. She has also published two poetry collections in Danish called "Dryppende Ord" and "Hunulven" in 2020 and 2021.

Louise writes with the power of poetry from the heart of a woman. Each poem telling a story of life lived. A primordial force of words which originate from generations of women through a bloodline of witches, mages, seers, and storytellers. The DNA from an underworld of magic and power.
Contact: louisesdigte@gmail.com

Louise Longson

25   **A Wolf in Poet's Clothing**
114   **Shroud**
129   **The jasmine flowers**   *(#haikuchallenge)*

Louise Longson started writing poetry in her late 50s, during isolation in lockdown 2020. She is published by One Hand Clapping, Fly on the Wall, Nymphs, Ekphrastic Review, Obsessed with Pipework, Indigo Dreams Publishing, Dreich, Black Bough Poetry, The Poetry Shed and others. She is the author of the chapbooks Hanging Fire (Dreich Publications, 2021) and Songs from the Witch Bottle: cytoplasmic variations (Alien Buddha Press, 2022). A qualified psychotherapist, she works remotely from her home in a small rural village for a charity that offers a listening service to people whose physical and emotional distress is caused by loneliness and historic trauma. Her poems are inspired by a bringing together of her personal and work experiences, myth and legend, and the natural environment. Find her on Twitter @LouisePoetical

Marilyn Timms

34   **CAFFEINE RUSH**
149   **Words that cannot be**   *(#haikuchallenge)*

Marilyn Timms has read her prize-winning stories and poems at six Cheltenham Literature Festivals. Alison Brackenbury described Poppy Juice as brave and unexpected adventures, with intoxicating, sometimes threatening colours. Marilyn's second collection is Deciphering the Maze (Indigo Dreams)

Marilyn is co-editor at wildfire words ezine and Frosted Fire books.

https://wildfire-words.com

Matty Blades

15	A billion
55	Forevermore
63	"Hello"
77	I'm gratefull, but there are still the lost
90	Metafalls
123	star burst haiku *(#haikuchallenge)*

I started writing poetry after the loss of my sister in 2001, first of all was a poem called Wings Of A Dove for her funeral, then I carried on as a journal in poetry form.

Gloucester Poetry Society have a special place in my heart being theirs was the first poetry group and open mic I'd ever attended, which helped my confidence immensely.

I've suffered addiction homelessness and poor mental health throughout my life, so when I can, I do try to give back helping those that have helped me to get where I am today.

Morgan (I'm not a Poet) Rye

106	Rule of Three
137	The vlogger, the baker, the mortgage maker

Very excited to see The Rule of Three in print (Quinn's poem). Inspired by my first novel, **Snowball Earth – Quinn**, due out late 2022/ early 2023. May I say this or is it advertising?

M. Palowski Moore (Silver Lion Poet)

60   GHOSTS OF THE DANUBE
121   SPIRIT DANCERS
143   WAITING

M. Palowski Moore is a poet, writer and storyteller. He has five volumes of poetry, including the Lambda Award nominee BURNING BLUE. His compositions reflect diverse themes and interpretations of prejudice, racism, socioeconomic inequality, homophobia and systemic oppression. He is the recipient of numerous accolades, including a Phi Beta Kappa Artistic Creation award for his collection of poems SILVER LION, awarded a Writer's Digest Certificate of Merit for the collection of poems KALEIDOSCOPE and a Sammy Davis,Jr./ Zora Neale Hurston Award for Arts and Humanities. He is a contributing poet to the Civil Rights Memorial Center (SPLC) community poem A CIVIL COMMUNITY, a new exhibit that will be featured inside the final gallery of The Civil Rights Memorial Center. In 1984, he served as a torchbearer in the 1984 Olympic Torch Relay.

https://facebook.com/silverlionpoet
Palowski Moore (@silverlionpoet) • Instagram photos and videos

Nick Lovell

54   Forever Marvellous
64   Here is what I have so far!
68   Hunt

Nick Lovell is a full-time optimist, part time poet and half arsed anarchist. He has won slams, performed at the Royal Albert Hall, performed as an open miker, support act, headliner and host at various events both in real time and online and has a book, Ever Since The Accident" published Black Eyes Publishing. He Co-hosts Oooh Beehive in Swindon alongside Clive Oseman.

Nupur Chakrabarty

43   **Crown**   *(#haikuchallenge)*
102   **Rampage**

My name is Nupur Chakrabarty. I am a post graduate in Psychology from the University of Delhi, India. I write poetry, since my childhood. As a poet I am very observant about the nature, people and society. I love reading a lot. I believe that there are truths beyond the worldly ones. And also, love and humanity together make the religion of the humans. My poems have been published in some journals and magazines in India and abroad. I got a little book-let published in the past too. I believe that true poetry and art can bring changes in the world.

https://www.facebook.com/profile.php?id=100010915634443

Peter Lay

42   **Covid – Day 8**

Peter Lay is a former youth worker, youth arts worker, international rock band manager and promoter. He now is now a publisher with the publishing house, 'Black Eyes' together with Josephine Lay.

He has co-written, with Zaiming Wang, a dual language (English/Chinese), cross cultural metaphorical conversation, 'Yellow Over the Mountain'.

He has visited Japan three times and during his trip last in November 2018, he experienced an emotional event when in Nagasaki and Hiroshima. Several poems about this are featured in his Poetry book, 'Still Tilting at Windmills' published in 2019.

Peter Lay ~ Performer, Promoter, Painter, Poet & Publisher
Facebook: Peter Lay
Blackeyespublishinguk.co.uk

Raine Geoghegan

108   SAINT SARAH THE PATRON SAINT OF THE ROMANI
                                                    PEOPLE

- **Her Names are Many**
- **Shrine at Saint Marie de la Mer**
- **Lucky 'eather**
- **The One**
- **Know My True Face**

Raine Geoghegan, poet and prose writer has an MA in Creative
Writing from the University of Chichester. Born in the Welsh Valleys,
she is of Romany, Welsh and Irish ethnicity. She has been nominated
for the Forward Prize; Pushcart Prize and the Best of the Net 2018. Her
poems and prose have been published online and in print with Under
the Radar; Poetry Ireland Review; The Clearing; Travellers' Times;
Skylight 47 and many more. Her work has been anthologised many
times and her essay, 'It's Hopping Time' was featured in the anthology
'Gifts of Gravity and Light' with Hodder & Stoughton. She has three
poetry chapbooks published with Hedgehog Press. Her First Full
Collection was published with Salmon Poetry Press in June 2022.

https://www.rainegeoghegan.co.uk/
Facebook - Raine Geoghegan
Twitter - RaineGeoghegan5
LinkedIn & Instagram – rainegeoghegan

Rebecca Mo

88   I Was A Teen

"I've loved words and writing since I was very young but it took me to
last year (at the grand old age of 33!) to share any of mine with
anybody else. And look where it got me - hello!"

Sally Aspden

19   **A graceful ballet**   *(#haikuchallenge)*
89   **Let the past dissolve**   *(#haikuchallenge)*
146   **Walking Meditation**

Sally Aspden was born in North Wales and has lived in Gloucester since 1999. She used to work as a software developer for the NHS, but is currently enjoying a career break. She loves reading and loves the natural world. She has written poetry on and off all her life, but more seriously in the last seventeen years.

Scott Cowley *(aka Rusty Goàt the Poet)*

30   **bitter over brewed tea**
57   **forgotten and forgettable**
84   **It's a work in fucking progress**
142   **Vomit**
144   **waiting waiting waiting...**

Scott Cowley (aka Rusty Goàt the Poet)
what would you like for breakfast?
words... my simple reply.

Simon Townsend

58   **Ghosts**

Sue Finch

33	Bring Me a Ladder
40	Cloudless sky, smoothed blue *(#haikuchallenge)*
125	Swinging
126	The Coin

Sue Finch's debut collection, 'Magnifying Glass', was published in 2020. Her work has also appeared in a number of online magazines. She lives with her wife in North Wales. She loves the coast, peculiar things and the scent of ice-cream freezers. You can often find her on Twitter @soopoftheday.

Sue Hubbard

37   Christmas
116   Silver Service

Sue Hubbard is an award-winning poet, freelance art critic and novelist. She has published four poetry collections. The most recent is Swimming to Albania from Salmon Poetry.

She has also published a collection of short stories and three novels. Her latest, Rainsongs, is available from Duckworth. Her fourth, Flatlands, is to be published by Pushkin Press in 2013, who are reissuing her second, Girl in White, on the life of Paula Modersohn Becker to coincide with the exhibition The Making of Modernism at the RA.

As the Poetry Society's only ever Public Art Poet, she was commissioned by the BFI and the Arts Council to create a poem leading to the IMAX from Waterloo. This is now being carved in stone by the artist Gary Breeze to be permanently placed in the crypt of St. John's Church, Waterloo.

www.salmonpoetry.com, www.duckworthbooks.com, www.pushkinpress.com, www.suehubbard.com, www.poetryarchive.org

Tish Ince Poet

26   A Year Like This
82   I polish shoes
103   Real Bed
112   Sewn on the bias

Tish Ince; London-born Trinidadian, Irish feminist, published poet based in San Francisco. Nominated for Gloucestershire Poet Laureate (2019), she also won a Paper Nations Award as Marginalised Writer (South West) in 2020. She has been recently compared to artist Kae Tempest and poet, Langston Hughes. She is a passionate and impassioned Black conscious poet and brings a modern lick to her take on fighting against racism and oppression. She writes page, performance and video poetry with musical spoken word in the US and performs in San Francisco and globally.

Trevor Valentine

138   Timber Cries

Guitarist, singer-songwriter, poet-in-training, Trevor Valentine has found a welcome refuge in poetry. With a foundation in English, French and Russian literature, just about to hit 65, ever realising life isn't a rehearsal. Poetry and songwriting is unfortunately not a tap you can just turn on, so, when the waters flow, enjoy. So pleased to be included in this selection alongside so many veritable poets.

Vicky Hampton

18   A Cold pale azure   *(#haikuchallenge)*
44   Cueva de las Manos, Argentina

Vicky Hampton is a Writing for Wellbeing facilitator. She runs bespoke poetry workshops, as well as a peer-learning poetry group, PIPs (Poets In Progress). Her work covers a wide rage of themes, often exploring the natural world or issues around family, loss and grief. Winner in various poetry competitions including the Welsh International, she is published in Graffiti, Red Poets, The Salopeot, Sarasvati magazines, and in the Ways to Peace and #MeToo anthologies, and the I Am Not A Silent Poet, Wildfire Words and The Poetry Village webzines. Vicky has appeared three times at Cheltenham Poetry Festival.

Z. D. Dicks

32   Bracing

Gloucestershire Poet Laureate

Black Eyes Publishing UK

'Black Eyes' is an independent publisher, based in sight of the cheese-rolling hill in Brockworth, Gloucestershire.

'Publishing from the Edge'

We were established in 2018. Our aims are to produce a small number of exciting, and at times, alternative literature in various genres.

'Quality not Quantity'

blackeyespublishinguk.co.uk

Lightning Source UK Ltd.
Milton Keynes UK
UKHW031033181022
410673UK00010B/513